BUILDING UP
THE
CHURCH

So with yourselves; since you are eager for spiritual gifts, strive to excel in them for building up the church.

—1 Corinthians 14:12

Table of Contents

Introduction

The Episcopal Church has been buffeted by change, controversy, even scandal, in the recent past. Reports from the media have given the impression that we have lost our mission to proclaim the good news of Jesus Christ.

But something else is now taking place. The decline in our membership has stopped and shows slow, solid progress. Many an Episcopal parish embodies clear excitement and enthusiasm, evidence that something fresh and new is in our midst.

When The Forward Movement was established by the General Convention meeting in Atlantic City in 1934, the original statement of mission included the words "to help reinvigorate the life of the church." This book is offered at the General Convention, meeting in Philadelphia in 1997, to capture today's new vigor through twelve different views of new life in the church.

The chapters that follow offer insightful commentary in twelve areas of our common life. The commentators, each involved in this new life, were chosen because of their particular understanding, expressed in a specific part of our common life. They offer stories, twelve windows, into the life of the Body of Christ, as it is experienced today in the Episcopal Church.

For a considerable period of time—twenty-five years—the Episcopal Church has been caught up in a period of adjustment and assessment. The internal life of the church has been marked by important and considerable changes. These changes have demanded abundant energy and attention, and during this period, membership growth has halted and declined. Forward movement was continued, but marked by indicators other than growth.

More recently many changes have been solidified, and growth and vitality in many Episcopal churches have again been signaled by the increased numbers of new members. Their presence is marked by critical indications of new life. The vitality is so real and discernible that it should be spread throughout the Episcopal Church.

This book is offered to show the skeptic that there is healthy new life in the church. It is offered to show the faithful new models of ministry that may help in their service to God. It is offered to the beleaguered as a way of demonstrating that creative ministry need not result in burn out. And last and most important, it is offered with the prayer that the Episcopal Church will continue to move forward in its mission to gather persons together in the power and presence of our Lord and Savior, Jesus Christ.

Edward Stone Gleason
Robert Murray Ross

CHAPTER I

Grow and Flourish

Some years ago I was leading a spiritual growth class for a small group of adults which included a young couple who were new to the church, together with their infant son. As I talked the infant was lovingly cradled in his mother's lap. The issue I was discussing was the importance, even necessity, for on-going personal spiritual growth. Suddenly, I stopped teaching, pointed to the mother and child and said, "Just look at that. What a charming picture of dependence and care! However," I continued, "if we were to return here in a year's time, and see the same mother with the same child and notice that there had been no change in the child—he had simply remained at the same stage of growth, then we would no longer consider this to be such a charming vignette but rather a tragedy. Something had gone terribly wrong in infant development and the child had experienced arrested growth." I then went on to say to this group, "This is the common tragedy afflicting many adult church members: they have experienced arrested spiritual development."

Recently, I began another series of spiritual

growth classes for adults. I have taught this particular series a number of times, but I go again. Why? Not simply because people continue to show up for the classes, but, more importantly, because I am convinced that encouraging personal spiritual growth is indispensable to the development of a healthy congregation.

If arrested spiritual growth is common or, worse, prolonged in a congregation, enthusiasm, excitement, and expectation are strikingly absent. This atmosphere is rapidly communicated to all new and prospective church members.

There are three issues that confront us if we are committed to on-going spiritual growth.

• What prevents people from continuing to experience personal spiritual growth?

• How could people most effectively be helped to grow in this way?

• What is the result of such spiritual growth?

Barriers to Spiritual Growth

Fear and ignorance are two of the most common barriers to spiritual growth. Sometimes the fear is misplaced—"I don't want to take spiritual growth seriously because I might become a religious fanatic who is an embarrassment to friends and an object of scorn to others." Cuthbert Beardsley, one-time Bishop of Coventry, once said somewhat ruefully, "Delirious enthusiasm is not the chief peril facing the English clergy." I think we can accurately apply these words to many average members of our congregations. Indeed, a significant amount of spiritual growth could occur in many Episcopal congregations before religious fanaticism became a threat.

Paul was a hard-driving young executive who was in my congregation in Cape Town, South Africa. As his faith developed from being fairly nominal, he told me how furious he was at God for bringing all this change into his life. "I told the Lord I would not give up my comfortable house and life-style and especially not my car." I would just listen to his diatribe and finally he would ask, "OK, how do I pray?"

Personal spiritual growth necessarily involves change. This is because for Christians spiritual growth is growth in Jesus Christ; in biblical terms it involves our becoming more conformed to the image of Christ. As this begins to occur, Jesus challenges our attitudes, priorities, behaviors, and speech—in short, every aspect of our lives. This is frightening and hard because it involves swimming against the stream of our culture. Of course, not all change is necessarily good, but if the challenge to change that we face is the result of a deepening faith in Christ and clearer understanding of the implications of such a faith, then we can be sure that change, while challenging and even demanding, will result in our long-term good and health.

Paul ultimately did give up his house, his car, and his life-style, but if you were to ask him today he would say without hesitation that the way he has been led by God since that time has more than made up for those things. Living as Christians is supposed to be an adventure. All too often our churches manage to communicate a total lack of expectation that the Living God is longing to act in our lives in ways which lead to challenge, growth, and wholeness. We settle for the predictability and order of the graveyard rather than the noise and excitement of the nursery.

How do people grow spiritually in Christ? For years I used to think that knowledge was the key. That is, if people are given sufficient information regarding theology, the Bible, spirituality, etc. then spiritual growth would automatically occur. I have come to see that there is much more to it than imparting propositional truths. One day I had an "epiphany" while leading a class in which I was presenting the evidence available to us which points to the truth of the bodily resurrection of Jesus. I was explaining that we are dealing with circumstantial evidence of the sort that does not necessarily compel belief but rather reassures people that they have good grounds to choose to believe. To illustrate, I pointed to the fact that there is a wealth of evidence linking smoking to lung cancer, emphysema and a host of other ailments, yet many smokers, the tobacco industry, and others profess themselves not to be convinced by the evidence. I was saying "You can lead a horse to water, but you can't make it drink" when I suddenly realized the inadequacy of knowledge alone to ensure spiritual growth. The essence of spiritual growth is change or transformation of people's characters, priorities and behaviors. It is a result of an experience of the Living God.

Cindy was a young woman who had recently begun to worship in the church I served in Cape Town. I asked her to tell me what had brought her to our church. She explained that she came from an

English upper-class background but had had no interest in the church for many years. She went on to explain that her husband had recently died under tragic circumstances. While scuba diving he had had a heart attack and drowned, leaving her with three young children. A couple of months before his death, because of financial difficulties with his business, he had canceled all his personal life insurance. Cindy went on to explain that two weeks after the funeral she discovered that she was pregnant with their fourth child. She then described how, through these unimaginably painful events, God had revealed himself to her and now she was looking for a church where she could get involved and continue her spiritual growth.

I sat there absolutely stunned by her story. For me that was a "moment of transendence" as I realized that clever arguments, words, and ideas simply did not cut it when the chips were really down. It was God himself who had touched her at a very deep part of her life.

While information may often be a component of such change, it is not the agent of change itself. St. Paul, reflecting on his proclamation of the Gospel and its impact in the lives of people said, "I planted, Apollos watered, but God gave the increase" (1 Corinthians 3:6). We humans can plant and water by giving means for growth and by providing nurture and expectation for growth—even by challenging people to respond to the implications of the Gospel by changing—but it is God by his Spirit who does the work of spiritual growth. Of course, such is the faithfulness of God that he is always much more ready to work in our lives and bring about spiritual growth than we are to let him.

Tools for Spiritual Growth

In over twenty years of ministry on three different continents, I have found that some of the most effective tools to help spiritual growth are: small groups, effective pastoral care, the varied circumstances of people's lives, and giving people opportunities to be "stretched" in their faith.

I do not believe that sustained personal spiritual growth is possible unless people are involved in a small group experience which involves prayer, accountability, community, and devotional Bible study (i.e. the reading of scripture in a prayerful and expectant manner where one is asking the question, What is God saying to us through this passage of scripture?). Perhaps my favorite service of the whole year is the one that we hold on Thanksgiving Day at which people have an opportunity to talk about ways that God has been working in their lives for which they are particularly thankful. What this does is to build a real sense of expectation that God is indeed active in other people's lives and, therefore, he can also be active in my life.

Part of pastoring people is not simply to offer "warm fuzzies" but to be ready to ask of them the question, What is God saying to you through what is presently happening in your life? In my experience, often it is in moments of pain and hardship that we are most able to hear the voice of God. Fred, a high-powered surgeon in one of the congregations

I served, was diagnosed with terminal lung cancer. I visited him and his wife immediately after the diagnosis. He was angry and frustrated and was asking God, "Why? Why have you let this happen to me?" I listened to him for a while and because I already had a close relationship with him finally took a deep breath and said, "Wrong question, Fred. The question that you need to be asking is not 'why?' but 'what?' 'What are you saying to me through this situation, God?'" I was afraid that he might throw me out, but instead he thought for a while and then quietly said, "OK, but will you help me discern the answer?" I visited him weekly for the next year and was present at his death. And during that time, as physically he wasted away, so spiritually he grew.

The Role of Obedience

On one occasion I was the rector of a church with a multiple staff and when I first arrived I proposed some changes which affected not only what I did but what other staff members did as well. One staff member on more than one occasion said to me, "We can't do this now because . . ." In a moment of frustration I said to her, "Jan, don't ask, just do it." Later that year Jan got to design T-shirts for the staff. When they arrived and were handed out, the words on the back were "Don't ask, just do it!"

The Epistle to the Romans begins and ends with the same phrase, "the obedience of faith" (1:3; 16:9). This is a powerful reminder that faith, far from being a tranquil or mystical feeling, is that which involves action. So often spiritual growth results when people are encouraged to "step out in faith," to allow themselves to be in a new place of dependency upon God. It's important to remember, however, that the obedience of faith means more than exercising our faith in mission and service; it also involves obedience within. It means allowing all aspects of our lives, our actions, behaviors, assumptions, and speech, as well as our characters to be sifted by the Spirit of God. This cannot happen unless we make the time to listen to God. This sifting by the Spirit can then lead to change in people as they display the obedience of faith. But to sustain that sort of obedience is almost impossible if we are trying to do it alone; we must be involved in a community where others are also committed to allowing that sort of sifting and transformation to occur. Without this, it is unlikely that we will stick with the program and in this context the critical role of small groups cannot be overemphasized.

The Goal of Spiritual Growth

The result of spiritual growth is not moving, mystical experiences, not further knowledge for knowledge's sake but on-going transformation. Such a process, although challenging, is also exciting and rewarding because it involves a growing awareness of involvement with God as he acts in our lives. As that occurs we experience an increasing sense of fulfillment and development. Spiritual growth is not some sort of optional extra, an avocation for a few enthusiasts; it is at the very heart of church life. Indeed, the purpose of the church, in addition to worship, is to be a community of Christ where growth, healing and transformation of its members occur.

The Rev. Ernest Ashcroft, Rector
St. Stephen's Church
Edina, Minnesota

CHAPTER II

On Church Growth

If one thing above all was true of the first Christians and their fledgling churches, it was that they were *alive*. After the darkness of the crucifixion and the mystery of the resurrection, the scattering uncertainty of Jesus' followers turned into a period of realization, powered by the Pentecost moment, that the Christ would live in what they came to call the Body of Christ.

To be alive a body must grow. That is the law of all living things. Health and life itself depend on growth. There is no no-growth option.

What follows are some observations and lessons learned by an amateur scientist of church growth. I say "scientist" because like many of us called to ministry I am unschooled in growth, but I am a restless experimenter.

Let me begin with a few observations on words and the Word and then recount some principles and experiences on the church growth front.

Biblical religion is quite literally *dynamic*. It's impossible to follow the narrative line of scripture without sensing movement and growth. Humankind exiled from the perfect garden. A people formed by exodus and wandering. Kingdom building followed by the rebukes of the prophets who smelled the rot of static, self-satisfied corruption. A Jesus community of proclamation and healing in the context of journeying, recruiting and preparing for a new community of journeying and growing.

Biblical Greek gives us "dynamic," the word behind "power" in Acts 1:8: "You will receive power when the Holy Spirit has come upon you." Dynamic means force or energy, marked by continuous, productive activity or change. That same New Testament Greek should inform our understanding of health. *Hygeia* means "living well," or more precisely, "a well way of living." *Euexia* means "well-habited-ness" or "good habit of body." English words for health all point to "wholeness" or "completeness," and however spiritually rich this notion can be, we have almost unconsciously let ourselves slide into an understanding of wholeness that is structural and static. The Greek words correctly point us to functioning and activity of the body—not only its working, but its working well.

Be sure to read often, and to teach clearly, how these understandings fueled the early church. Paul and his successors and colleagues richly put this language to work in their descriptions of mission and growth and in their teaching about it. Ephesians 4:11ff. speaks of "building up the body" and of the "whole body working properly." Colossians 1:16 and 2:19 make clear that growth is not just biological but firmly based on the Christ.

Remember, too, that growth is mysteriously

cumulative; and even the committed, converted soldier of growth is likely to benefit (or suffer) from others' work. Paul, who wasn't always modest, writes engagingly about this in 1 Corinthians 3:5-15. To grow, leaders must have a clear-eyed knowledge of their congregation's past and its personalities.

And of course Jesus' own teaching constantly uses growth parables (especially the Sower in Matthew 13:3ff. and its parallels) and his ministry repeatedly challenges his disciples to fish for people, seek the lost, and prepare for the challenges of a growth-focused ministry. He collected a growing number of followers, he "trained" successors, and he preached a growing kingdom.

I see no reason to think that our task is any different.

A word about numbers. Increasing numbers do matter. Obviously they measure the reach of our work. They are indicators of whether the body is healthy because it is growing or sick because its organic functions are beginning to shut down. But church leaders, and clergy especially, are often heard putting down any emphasis on growth in numbers. Undeniably, and for a lot of complex reasons, "mainline" churches like ours have seen an erosion of our share of the population. Rather than argue about the facts, or argue about causes, why not establish growth as a goal, embracing it as faithfulness to the Great Commission and as commitment to the living health of our beloved institution?

You still hear leaders—clergy, especially—defend small and declining numbers by saying that numbers are not really the point. I fail to see what glory there is in the rationalization that if we're growing in numbers we are somehow into people-pleasing and peddling cheap grace. Isn't it just possible that growth and trouble *should* go together? "Disturbing the comfortable," which many of us clergy have taken to be a litmus test of our own courage and integrity, often looks a lot like taking stands on "issues." Might it not also look like squeezing the pew sitters to make room for their neighbors? I seem to be in at least as much trouble when the congregation is growing as when it is static. So herewith a first principle:

There is always resistance to growth. Members of a body will resent the strategies that lead to growth, namely, the kind of preaching and worship that appeals to the seeker and attention paid to nonmembers. In a moment of grace (meaning that I had run out of clever answers and had tired of being defensive), I was able to reply to a good friend who exploded one Sunday after the service. We were going through a noticeable growth spurt. "I don't know anyone here anymore. I had to fight for a seat. And they don't even know how to use the prayer book!" "You know, I don't know everyone anymore either, Tom, and if you and I did know them all, this parish would be stuck and ready to decline and die."

Hallowed habits keep us small:

• The pastoral model of the priest as caretaker—or even a team of ministers primarily offering empathy—seems to ensure putting maintenance over mission. Good pastoring is Biblical and indispensable, but we need to rethink how we do it, or else we will continue caring for a disappearing flock.

• The prayer book is not enough. We have a fine

liturgy, and a book that makes it easy (for the professionals, at any rate) to open it and "do" it—week after week. Attracting people who are unchurched, unfamiliar with liturgy, or turned off by various church memories or associations requires user-friendly bulletins, the best music we can offer (regardless of style), and constant evaluation and improvement. For God to be glorified, Jesus preached and the Spirit present to enliven the proceedings, we must work, work, work to get the mechanics, the distractions and the mediocrities out of the way.

• I'm all in favor of the essential mystery of the religious "transaction." But in most of our churches, getting there is almost impossible. Do an audit on the barriers. Our signage, our advertising, our ushering, our child care, our sound systems, our coffee, our seats, our lights—I could go on—need improvement.

• Long services are killing the church in many places. A Eucharist with music, real preaching and hundreds coming to communion, can be done beautifully in an hour. It requires work, coordinating and discipline. People will forgive longer services on special occasions. They will be more likely to come to other venues for teaching and mission and group life if we don't wear them out at the primary event.

Large and growing churches are staff-intensive. To the greatest extent your current congregational size will permit, get the vestry out of the program business, where everyone seems to wear a departmental hat. Adopt the older, focused model of vestry purpose: to raise support of the mission (and plan long-range), to maintain the fabric and the property, and to call a rector. Through Bible study and learning about the church growth movement, convert the vestry to the big picture. Recruit and empower professionals for day to day operations. This will leave wide berth for just about any model of lay ministry and involvement. Keep the staff highly disciplined and focused on worship, clear communication, continuous improvement of what is offered, and constant removal of stumbling blocks. A corollary, of course, is that the rector focus on a very few things. Nothing empowers everyone else more than such powerful and humble focus in their leader.

Learn what you can from the "new church" or "mega church" movement. Our job is more difficult than that of the pastor or team who invent a congregation from the ground up. But surely we can remain faithful to our theology and our traditions and still learn from those who have aggressively sized up their markets and really thought about the realities of church-going in this society. Few of us would want the somewhat plastic feel and consumerist obsession of these churches, but we can imitate some of their focus, their commitment to constant evaluation of what they're doing, and their regard for the non-churched. All those elements, it seems to me, are essential for growth.

I have read quite a few parish mission statements in recent years. Most adopt some form of the baptismal covenant or offer a variation on the theme "to know Christ and make Christ known." Well and good. But if we are to become a growth-oriented denomination, we will need to be more explicit about using, without apology, the word growth in what we proclaim of our purpose. And to do that, we'll have to understand, believe and convert to growth in parish after parish.

The Rev. William M. Tully, Rector
St. Bartholomew's Church
New York, New York

CHAPTER III

Newcomers

*Do not neglect to show hospitality to strangers, for
thereby some have entertained angels unawares.*
—Hebrews 13:2

Since its inception in 1987, St. Anthony on the Desert
Episcopal Church, Scottsdale, Arizona, has never
been able to neglect this biblical mandate. Situated
in what a March, 1986, *Wall Street Journal* article
described as "one of the four fastest growing neighborhoods in the United States," St. Anthony's has
been welcoming the stranger as a matter of course
for nine years. Begun as a mission of the diocese
with 35 parishioners who met in a local school room,
today it has an average Sunday attendance of over
200 at three services. The current building will become a parish hall after the construction of a
500-seat nave, scheduled for completion in Decem-
ber, 1997.

It may seem ironic that this parish, so deft at
welcoming the stranger in its midst, is named for
St. Anthony of Egypt, that monk who sold everything

upon hearing the gospel story and fled to the desert to live in a cell as a hermit. What many forget, however, is that others followed him. He is well known for providing hospitality in the desert, meeting the physical as well as the spiritual needs of the desert monks who looked to him as Abba. In one instance, he took a monk with him on a day's journey. At the end of that day, he marked the spot and decided that this would be a logical place to build a monastery so that monks could carry the message of Jesus Christ to new terrain and yet be comforted along the way.

And so it is with our parish, founded by the Diocese of Arizona to meet the needs of settlers in the northeastern corner of the "Valley of the Sun" in metropolitan Phoenix. The primary mission of the church is to grow as it tells the Good News. The Good News is not merely told to the converted but to the unchurched as well.

St. Anthony's has consistently welcomed the stranger with a program of hospitality. Since so many parishioners are from other sections of the country, St. Anthony's has been a center of welcome and stability for others who move here or those whose lives are in the midst of major transitions. In a place deemed to be isolating and lonely, St. Anthony's has served as a center of building community and forging new friendships. The parish has accomplished this in a variety of ways.

Small groups meet varying needs of the congregation. A play group for young moms and dads meets on Fridays. Several newcomers have been introduced to the group, which provides interaction for children

Building Up the Church

as well as fellowship for the adults. One mother recently concluded that play group is the highlight of her week, a way to meet others in a new town and a means to overcome the isolation so often felt by parents of small children. Another group, fourteen parishioners who are residents of a nearby retirement community, gather Sunday morning to board a shuttle to church. They welcome other newcomers by offering them rides. Plans are underway to gather retired people during the week to share their concerns.

Scottsdale is composed of many senior citizens who are new to the area. They form a group who are churched and experienced leaders of congregations from across the nation. Newcomers are welcomed and are quickly recruited as leaders, but not so quickly as to overwhelm them! The key is that St. Anthony listens to the needs of newcomers and attempts to address them.

A steering committee of thirty parishioners, who serve for one-year terms, is actively interested in newcomers. Newcomers committees are too often burned out by long terms and tasks that are too onerous. Clergy support is vital, but laypersons are the front line contact with newcomers.

The St. Anthony Newcomer's Committee has three foci: first, Sunday morning greeters and hospitality providers at coffee hour; second, a team that delivers a St. Anthony's kit to newcomers by Thursday following their first Sunday; third, a group that sponsors a quarterly newcomer reception centered on the reality that established parishioners have much in common with newcomers. Who better to assess the needs of newcomers than someone in the midst of the experience? St. Anthony's has new parishioners who have been active elsewhere and are eager to be leaders. The Newcomer's Committee is an ideal place for their involvement.

The Newcomer's Committee represents the parish, but its work demands that all parishioners be actively involved in the welcoming process. Since all are newcomers, all feel a duty to welcome others. This can be a lesson for more mature congregations. The welcome extended to the newcomer is often subtle, one that neither intimidates newcomer nor parishioner. It is a quiet witness to God's love for the stranger newly arrived to the parish, rather than a marketing blitz. This is an important distinction in this era of the mega-church that emphasizes business marketing practices.

Each person who enters the nave on Sunday morning receives a service leaflet that contains all the words of the service, including the hymns. Early in each service there is an official word of welcome, and at this time all worshipers are asked to prepare a simple name tag and wear it. Newcomers are asked to identify themselves, and greeters lead them to the coffee hour and ask for the necessary information to include them on the parish mailing list.

For the entire parish, welcoming the newcomer is more a matter of active listening than telling, more a matter of doing what is simple than what is complicated. Groups such as the Stephen ministers and individual parishioners on their own initiative offer information concerning the new community, as well as a listening heart to the newly-arrived parishioner. St. Anthony's strives to offer a living, breathing, welcoming picture of the Body of Christ to the stranger in our midst.

Bringing newcomers into the community of the faithful means growth, and this can produce anxiety. At St. Anthony's this anxiety has been reduced by remembering that we are not, and cannot be, in control of the process. The church is meant to carry its message into the world and to grow. The Holy Spirit will nurture that growth; it is not for the people of the parish to stifle the work of the Holy Spirit.

As growth continues, the parish will strive to keep the small church atmosphere. Toward this end, staff has been increased, more small group programs have been created, and house Eucharists take place to forge closer ties.

The parish is already planning that one day St. Anthony's will establish a mission church in an outlying area, just as it was once established. Welcoming the newcomer is a never-ending task, one that extends beyond our own walls. We believe that at St. Anthony's, as we welcome people to the parish, we welcome them also to the diocese, the province and to the national Episcopal Church.

The Rev. Gerald C. Anderson, Rector
The Rev. Daniel H. Schoonmaker, Associate
St. Anthony on the Desert
Episcopal Church
Scottsdale, Arizona

CHAPTER IV

Outreach as the Vocation for Being a Parish

The rays of the morning summer sun first hit the feet of the banner of Our Lady of Guadelupe, then move slowly to warm the black crucifix of Escapulas and then on to the Asian altar with the seated image of the Buddha before the icon of Quan Yin. At the same time the lingering smell of sweet grass and sage begins to stir as the abalone shells are warmed across the sanctuary at the American Indian altar surrounded by eagle feathers, a turtle rattle and medicine sticks.

The Parish of St. Philip the Deacon is the regional parish of East San Jose, California, comprising five distinct ethnic/cultural worshiping communities with nine primary languages. The ministry evolves through a series of partnerships between each community and the larger society. In some cases partnerships have resulted in creating an agency, institution or association to serve thousands of people who would not be drawn into the Episcopal Church.

In the late '70s I was in a continuing education class for Episcopal clergy at the Church Divinity School of the Pacific. Jim McClintock, an American Baptist professor, threw us a challenge: "I have yet to find an Episcopal priest who understood the great advantage you have over all the other denominations in this country. Your Anglican heritage assumes the structure of the geographic parish and the position of being the established church. The dark side of this is the elitism that has plagued you for centuries. But the positive side is a deep sense that your corporate vocation is to serve *all sorts and conditions of people*—everyone living within the boundaries of each parish. They belong to the cure of the local Episcopal Church. Other denominations identify who is their responsibility by clear definitions of membership. But a truly Anglican response is to affirm that everyone living in the geographical location is in the parish, regardless of faith orientation."

This confirmed for me the manner in which ministry was flowing for St. Philip's. Increasingly I had found something artificial about the term "outreach" because it gave the congregation the option to reach out or not. Either the church demonstrates that the whole of creation is interconnected or it falls into the dominant ethos of selfishness and isolation. This challenge came at a pivotal moment and reflected the shift in attitudes at St. Philip's. The evolution was toward a more inclusive sense of ministry by pursuing partnerships with other groups in order to serve the larger community.

As the parish entered the '80s we began to pray intentionally for new members. Little did we know that those who were to come would not look like the majority of African-American and Euro-American members who had been attracted to this ministry since 1957. These new people would be representative of the changing east side, where the local high schools today have an average of 98 primary languages spoken among the students.

In the summer of 1981 two Laotian families arrived in the parish while I was on sabbatical. They had come from St. Alban's in Albany, California, who had sponsored them as refugees. They were encouraged to come to St. Philip's because of its openness. They began taking communion even though they obviously did not understand English. Dorothy Curry, the seminarian in charge of the parish, was not sure what to do. The overload of theological education set off bells in her when she saw that some Lao were wearing Buddhist amulets as they extended their hands for the bread and wine. She called the bishop and asked him what to do. He said, "Baptize them!" She called me, explained what had happened and what the bishop had said. My reply was direct, "Don't you dare! We are not going to do what missionaries have done for centuries: baptize people without their understanding what they were entering into. But don't prevent them from coming for Communion!"

Three years later, with 120 Lao related to the parish, 20 were baptized, confirmed and received. By then we had translators that worked with Barbara Somers, a lay catechist. She discovered that half of the Lao were Roman Catholic and that they knew exactly what they were doing when they first attended in 1981. On the Sunday of the baptisms Shannon Mallory, the Bishop of El Camino Real, set aside his regular sermon to talk, through translators, about the statue of the Buddha on the side altar. He said that the presence of the Lao in this parish represented immense gifts of spiritual depth and a tradition of meditation from Buddhism that were being brought into the Anglican Communion. He concluded by saying that when the statue of the Buddha moves from the side altar to a more central place in the sanctuary we will know that a fuller integration of Eastern and Western spirituality has been reached.

This has become the pattern of ministry development for St. Philip's: partnership and bridge building with other communities. The greater part of the refugee Lao community (6,000 in Santa Clara County) remain Buddhist but many consider St. Philip's their "church home."

From the arrival of the Lao the model of partnership ministry has continued to expand to include Latinos, primarily from Guatemala and Nicaragua; Filipinos, Hawaiians, East Indians, and American Indians representing 17 tribes. Under the leadership of one of the associate rectors, Sylvestre Romero, who is now Bishop of Belize, two additional Latino congregations came into existence in the diocese. Through the partnership efforts of St. Philip's, Chinese and Korean congregations were formed in other parishes. The Filipino ministry is now a separate mission of the diocese.

The first two decades of the parish had seen more traditional "outreach and social ministries": refugee resettlement, civil rights involvement, housing issues, migrant workers, development of social service agencies, food banks and emergency services. In the '70s there was a shift toward creating partnerships in order to respond to the underserved of our community. The initial partnership included participating in the formation of two nonprofit corporations: a crisis counseling center for youth and their families that by 1985 was seeing 5,000 youths per year, and a Montessori multicultural pre-school with a third of the students being subsidized and coming from low income families. Fifteen primary languages are spoken by the children. Over the years several million dollars have been awarded to these institutions by the county, state, and federal governments.

Now this may appear as a logical development, but it is far from it. St. Philip's had to begin, and continues, to go through a process of transformation, evolving as the society changes. It has been a process of death and rebirth over and over again. One of the most painful processes has been for the existing leadership at each stage of partnership building to reach a point where they have to let go of their control. Even with the best of intentions there comes a point where the initiating leadership stands in the way of future development.

Fluidity is a hallmark of this ministry development. There is an ebb and flow in partners' relations. Everyone has had to face their prejudices or else the ministry would be derailed. Experimentation and imagination are premium tools. There are five primary times of weekly worship, with occasional feast days, where all of the parish is encouraged to come together. According to the bylaws of the parish the vestry consists of four junior wardens representing the principal congregations, a senior warden, and four at-large members who have been nominated with inclusive representation in mind. From the early '80s it became important to communicate to the Lao, Latinos, Filipinos, American Indians, African-Americans and Euro-Americans that they were equal partners in the parish and were entitled to a principal seat on the vestry.

The term "outreach" doesn't appear often in conversations at St. Philip's, but "partnerships" with the world is a constant point of reference. We are trying to draw a circle in which we understand that we share a responsibility to all who live within the parish boundaries—with other Christian congregations and parishes, Buddhist temples and monasteries, Sikh temples and mosques, as well as social agencies and institutions who seek to care and support the lives of families and individuals on the east side.

Some people are shocked when they come into the parish center of St. Philip's and see the five ethnic altars that line the walls of the sanctuary. The focus of worship, however, is on the square central altar, called the Jerusalem altar because of a square stone from the rock formation of Golgatha imbedded in the top. As the congregation gathers, especially at an all-parish Eucharist, people look around the circle. Then the familiar anthem is spoken and the words ". . . gathered from every tribe, people and nation . . ." and the setting make sense. These side altars are not so much separate places of worship, but forms of stained glass windows representing thresholds and the heritages through which each of the members has passed—American Indian, Hawaiian, African-American, Latino, Asian-American, Asian Indian, and Euro-American.

Leadership is everything. The pattern of partnership is most clearly seen in the relationship of lay and clergy leaders. The key players have had to develop a sense of trust with each other and maintain open communications, periodically renewing the vision together as ministry development evolves in each area. It is this networking across cultural norms and dynamics that is the most challenging but most rewarding in the life of St. Philip's.

The Rev. Jerry W. Drino, Rector
St. Philip's Church
San Jose, California

CHAPTER V

The Fabric of a Congregation

Church shopping is a common modern phenomenon. Those who move to a new community or have their life jarred by transition or lose enthusiasm for their previous congregation make up the core of the browsers. After a Sunday morning reconnoiter shoppers can be heard to say, "This place is not like old St. Paul's where I grew up," or "This is OK, but it is not exactly what I am looking for," or "As soon as I walked in I knew that this was the place for me." Few of them know the term, but what they are remembering, looking for and finding is the fabric of congregational life.

Fabric is what one has when all of the pieces are knit together. As with cloth, it is all that touches the senses and more. In a parish it is the obvious elements of parking, seating, symbols, colors, grounds, choirs, sermons and ritual. And it is the presence or absence of smiles, mink coats, laughter, silence and certain age groups. In addition it is the subtle interplay of the focus of prayers, the implications of announced activities, attendance at coffee hour, the message of the messages on bulletin boards, friendliness and cleanliness as well as Godliness. At a deeper level it is the degree to which people are on a spiritual journey or in a mighty fortress. It is about openness and vulnerability, the depth of conversations, the content as well as the civility of disagreements, the kind of listening that happens and the expectations people have of God's action in their individual as well as corporate lives.

There was a time when the fabric of a congregation was not as important as it is now. The character of congregations used to reflect the culture in which they were located. This was especially true of Episcopal churches which had a brief moment but a lingering memory of being a state church. In small towns and stable neighborhoods there was an apparently seamless fabric that stretched across school, church and civic life. The three terms were used almost as a single word. In such an environment the unique qualities of a congregation did not stand out. Those days are gone in most communities. The church's scouts such as Loren Mead, Stephen Carter, Will Willimon, Stanley Hauerwas, *et al.* have been reporting that the times are changing and that relationship between church and culture is changing with it. Just as schools used to play a supporting role to a consistent concept of family and community life but now must provide meals, teach hygiene, baby-sit and otherwise replicate the function of a family, so, too, the church used to play a role in society but now must be a society in and of itself.

Churches in the evangelical wing of protestantism have always had to do it, but now mainline congregations are required to become self-sustaining villages of faith in a world different or hostile to their enterprise and even existence. The prevailing culture no longer articulates its morality in theological terms. The stories of faith are not passed on through any medium other than the church. As society divides itself into ever more refined specialties, the congregation remains the only place in town that cares about every aspect of a person's life. The parish priest is the last generalist. Because of this each congregation has had to figure out its identity apart from, and sometimes even over against, its surrounding culture. Christ Church, Central City, now has to understand itself more by the first two words of its title than the last two. In this environment Episcopal and other mainline congregations are becoming more aware of the importance of their unique and special fabric.

Because the fabric of a parish involves the whole of its life, the clergy are in the best position to observe it. Any church shopper can sense it, but the clergy who have the combination of time, expertise, exposure and responsibility have the best chance of understanding and articulating it. One of the primary responsibilities of the parish priest today is to enable the congregation to deal purposefully with its fabric, because in the final analysis it is the fabric, the whole of the congregational life, that bears witness to Jesus Christ.

The ordained have a key role to play in understanding the fabric of congregational life but the real makers of that fabric are the baptized ministers, a.k.a. the laity. According to the Clergy Deployment Office, a rector's normal length of stay is seven years. That is plenty of time to know the fabric of a congregation but not enough time to change it in any significant way. The issue of fabric must be addressed jointly by the ordained who can describe it and the baptized who can change it.

Intentionally crafting the fabric of a parish is one of the higher forms of both growth and evangelism. A congregation that is deepening its common life so that its programs bite into life, its rituals are rooted in meaning, its hopes give shape to people's lives and its outreach changes both givers and receivers, is growing in Spirit whether its numbers go up or down. Such a congregation will be evangelistic in at least the same way as the first congregation in Jerusalem was when Luke described it in Acts 2:46-47: "Day by day, they spent much time together in the temple, they broke bread at home and ate their food with glad and generous hearts, praising God and having the goodwill of all the people. And day by day the Lord added to their number those who were being saved." To be a suitable place for God to send those whom God is saving is the most basic step in being an evangelistic parish.

Fabric has been discussed for years. Church shoppers do it instinctively. Clergy know about "good congregations" and about those that shoot their wounded and eat their young. Baptized ministers involved in diocesan life come to know the reputations of various parishes. Terms such as "charismatic," "high church," "liberal," "'28 prayer book" and "social" are all used to indicate fabric. For the most part reputations and catch phrases are inadequate and do not express the full life of a congregation. Mission statements are popular institutional attempts to say what the fabric of a parish is like, but they are generally the result of compromise in committee and rarely say anything that distinguishes one congregation from another. Because the fabric of each congregation is unique, it does not lend itself to easy descriptions, but there are some questions that those who would understand it might be prepared to answer.

Who really owns this Church? We would all say that Christ is the true owner of any Christian church, but is there anything we would like to do, but do not, because of Jesus? Is there anything we would prefer not to do, but do anyway, because we are Christians? These questions can be considered by looking at the budget, the parish calendar, the issues being addressed by study groups, the reading material in the narthex and the guest speakers invited. If Christ is head of the church then the church should be different from what it would be if we were the head.

What do we disagree about and how do we handle it? If we say we do not have disagreements in our parish then we are denying some important piece of reality. As a wag once said, "When two people agree on everything, one of them is not necessary." God went to a lot of trouble to make each of us different. If those differences do not emerge in our parish life, we are staying pretty close to the surface. Disagreements are to be valued not only for the depth of relationship they imply but also for the greater truth which can be found through them. A good disagreement, well conducted with honesty, vulnerability and expectation, can make relationships stronger.

How do newcomers experience our congregation? They have an objectivity that members will lack and represent a reality that must be considered. "The way we do it at St. John's" may be obvious and comforting to the initiated but confusing and diminishing for those God is trying to bring into fellowship. The ties that bind also exclude. Consider asking a friend from out of town to visit your church on a Sunday and then tell you what the experience was like.

How have we changed in the last five years? One of the wonderful things about the kingdom of God is that every place in it is a good place to be. One of the mysteries of it is that there are no stopping places. Are we on a journey? Are people's lives being changed by our congregational life? Are the good people becoming better people?

What do we pray about? What is the Sunday prayer list likely to include? Do people express their concerns and vulnerabilities in requests for congregational prayers? Do we always pray for other people who live far away or are our prayers allowed to work close to home? What prayers are offered before meetings and by whom? Are the clergy the "designated pray-ers" in every situation or do others play that role as well? Do our prayers make any difference? To whom and how? What would happen if we did not pray as a community?

Who are the spiritual leaders in the congregation? What difference do they make in our common life? Are new spiritual leaders being raised up? How do people learn and grow as spiritual leaders?

Does our budget reflect our stated priorities? As one social critic put it, "Any organization that spends 70 percent of its talk on changing the world and 70 percent of its money on buildings has got to be hypocritical." Another way to think of it is that what we want to believe is recorded in our prayer books and what we really believe is recorded in our check books. This question can be raised for individual members as well for the parish as a whole.

In dealing with the fabric of congregational life, as with other important areas of life and faith, one is better prepared with good questions than with good answers. A congregation that wonders about these and similar questions and looks expectantly to the Holy Spirit for responses to them can expect to deepen its life. And more importantly, to be a suitable place for God to send those who are being saved.

The Rev. Francis W. Wade, Rector
St. Alban's Parish
Washington, DC

CHAPTER VI

Pastoral Care: the Work of the Whole Parish

"One evening last summer, members of the mission committee sat around Elizabeth Robinson's dining table and gave thanks for this parish full of people who nourish us with moments of God's presence through laughter and wisdom and compassion."

That was a quotation from a parish publication called *Advent 1993*. All Saints', Atlanta, solicited and published what parishioners said about remembered moments of grace. The statements were brief, candid and personal. They named people, expressed thankfulness for gifted moments and they pointed to God in our midst. Collectively, the testimonies were inspirational meditations that many, many people praised. But the publication did more than inspire. It taught. It focused the parish's attention on that most compelling teacher, our own experience. Writers looked into their own lives and said, "here is grace." Pepper Duncan wrote, "She didn't try to fix me or cheer me up. She simply let me be who I needed to be then . . . I'm not sure that I had ever felt accepted and as cared for as I did at that moment . . . later I tried to apologize for my tears. She said, 'Pepper, if we can't show each other our brokenness, how can we be the body of Christ for each other?'"

In this parish and throughout the church, pastoral care has been enriched by its attention to actual experience. There has been much personal and professional growth. What is lived is what is taught. These brief personal testimonies mean a lot. Priests are privy to wonders that most parishioners only occasionally see. We priests not only talk about new life, sometimes we see it. In the privacy of pastoral offices we have worked with those who have struggled with death and the demonic. We are witnesses of salvation.

Fortunately, there are those who write and give voice to experienced realities. Like gospel music that is spoken rather than sung, the writers declare to all that "There is a balm in Gilead." I have seen it in this place.

"The sea of people that came to us and helped hold us up. They were our families, dearest friends, neighbors, strangers, other bereaved parents and children. They came and called and cooked and took charge. They cried with us and for us and tried to get us to eat something . . . It is still amazing and ironic to me that at the worst time of my life, I felt more profoundly cared for than I ever had before." Jeanne Bedell wrote that in *Advent 1993*.

Families, friends, neighbors, strangers, the bereaved, children—are these the faces of God? While it comes as no surprise to most, it is still a fact that amazes. The channels of grace that the writers most often cite are lay people rather than clergy with training or without training, in or out of the community of faith; those who most often provide needed care are lay people rather than clergy. Our experience, collectively, tells us that pastoral care is the work of all the people.

Robert Stansell, writing in *The Parish Paper* of May, 1993, said "The day before my IV port was planted, Ann Woodall sensed I was upset. She's a busy person, but she stopped to ask me what was wrong. When I told her, she put her hand on my shoulder and said, 'Bob, whatever happens, you have left your legacy here.' That was one of the nicest things that anyone ever said to me in my whole life." For the overworked priest that's good news. For the parishioner who hesitates to receive a lay visitor, the idea may be perplexing. Yet the lay among us are affirmed. By name they are remembered and cited with thanksgiving. All Saints' is among that thankful group. Blessed with so many able lay people who willingly serve the parish as well as the larger community, the parish lives a collaborative life. From the senior staff to vestry and ministry committees, we are staffed to experience the conflict and joy of cooperative ventures.

Of course, staffing is intentional. It is a creature of leadership. We don't generally think of it as a program or a process, yet it is both. It is a parable that is created to mirror and challenge the parish to live out the Gospel. Lay and clergy are engaged for all to see and encounter. Through it leaders are called forth, around it the community is formed, and from it new initiates emerge. Sometimes staffing it works. Sometimes it doesn't. When it works it is who we are. When it doesn't it is still our community. Fundamentally, it is not a program, process or strategy that makes a parish vital; it is the community's life together.

Before their new rector arrived, but with his approval, the vestry of All Saints' once made two crucial pastoral decisions. First, they decided to redecorate the church. In a bold move they chose a design that featured brilliant colors, red and gold. The apse became warm, supportive and pastoral. Strangers are often rendered speechless. Parishioners, despite having lived with the change for years, speak of it with awe. No one dares discuss pastoral care at All Saints' without calling attention to the lay-conceived environment that invites all to come and rest.

The vestry's second decision was to accept the application of Integrity to use All Saints' facilities for meetings. Already sensitive to justice and civil rights issues, the vestry honored the request that many others would have rejected. The vestry understood that as other gays and lesbians came to use All Saints' facilities, many would choose to become members. The vestry had again made a bold pastoral decision, one that urban churches are most privileged to face. Within the city, there are so many encounters with people who differ that, over time, tolerance is given a chance to grow. Robert Stansell wrote, "When I came to All Saints', I knew only one person. But people were so nice. I remember the first heterosexual couple I met the first day I attended; they were sitting behind me, Barbara and Bill Anderson, and they were just so welcoming and interested in me. So many other people have been like that."

With a history and leadership that desire the whole church to serve and celebrate as one, All Saints' has flourished. Within Education for Ministry (EFM), foyer, singles, college, youth, seniors, novel theology and Disciples of Christ in Community (DOCC) groups, women's circles, newcomers, parish, transportation and hospital visitors, vestry and ministry committees and a host of other small groups, mutuality is made possible and collaboration and care happen.

Even Sunday's worship contains the minds of many. Each week, clergy, musicians, vergers, supervisors for the sextons, lectors, acolytes, ushers and altar guild, secretaries who type the worship bulletins, church school and youth leaders, gather to critique the service of the previous week and to arrange worship for the next Sunday. The meetings are lively events and the worship that is planned is repeatedly called outstanding.

With emphasis on exquisite music and preaching, the Sunday Eucharist is a weekly celebration that unites and invigorates the community. It is truly an "alive" experience of all the people. Spontaneous laughter or applause or tears might happen at any time. And though Sunday schedules are tight, there is always time to read the names and offer prayers for those who are ill and those 50 to 60 persons who celebrate birthdays. Few seats are ever vacant. New-comers arrive each Sunday.

In an Ash Wednesday sermon in 1996, the Rev. James D. Curtis said, "I want to thank All Saints' for what this parish has meant to me over the years. I first slipped into a pew here in 1970—just after a death in my family . . . this was a safe place for me to sit and grieve . . . There is a very healing tone about this place—about the clergy and people—a kind of healing hospitality, especially in the preaching . . ."

A community's culture does not happen out of the blue. It is rooted in a tradition, remembered by a few, and made relevant by the community leaders. It is a living force that energizes or it is a memory that paralyzes. Every community has its own stories to live.

All Saints' has been blessed with a saga of caring and performance that does well what is needed, when it is needed, for as long as it warrants the parish's attention. There are several institutions in Atlanta which were originally All Saints' ministries. Once they were firmly established and operating, All Saints' has historically withdrawn.

Of course life in the city is never that neat. Before one matter is settled, five other issues clamor for attention. Reality has a way of making its presence felt. It sometimes twists our best ideas so much that our actions bear little resemblance to what we planned. In my former life as an army chaplain, I remember a pastoral plan that seemed so right yet proved to be premature. Many years ago, for twenty-six busy days, our unit sailed toward Vietnam. Church services, Bible studies, talent shows and card games filled the time and answered great anxiety among us. Out of our prayers together there emerged a plan to care for each other, especially when we could no longer care for ourselves. Small prayer groups were formed in each unit and each person received copies of prayers to use with or for a comrade in the hour of his death. We made a covenant that no one's body would be left behind and everyone's faith would be honored by a suitable prayer.

The plan reassured. However, it didn't take long for the groups to disappear. Casualties happen quickly and replacements neither shared our boat experience nor knew of our commitments. So our program ended just a few months after it began. Soon what we did together in a boat became less important than what was being lived in combat. With life so contingent, community formed among peers rather than among those who regularly gathered to worship. Caring became the unit's concern rather than a responsibility of those of faith. Informally, promises were made and assurances were given. No one would be left behind. While few talked about saying suitable prayers, there was little doubt that each soldier would be honored by his peers. The plans we developed on a boat were birth pangs of a caring community born from the realities of a soldier's life. It didn't work the way we planned, because we grew.

Parishes don't live in vacuums, either. They not only influence but are shaped by the world around them. Atlanta has new institutions because All Saints' is here. But All Saints' is not the same, either.

It has been molded by many crises, two recently.

In the early eighties it was homelessness, and homelessness changed All Saints'. Before shelters were common and before there was suitable parish space, All Saints' opened its doors and the parish, supported by volunteers from other churches, hosted those who came. It was a daring effort that rallied the attention and support of the entire parish. While the city welcomed it and the homeless used it, parishioners grew to need it. People need to care, to contribute and enjoy common ventures. The shelter provided all three. Like home building with Habitat for Humanity and serving water to strangers during the Olympics, doing good in concert with others can be exhilarating and satisfying. Fittingly, those ministries that most people enjoy are also the activities that are shared with those outside the church. Sometimes the church is a sign of community wanting to be born.

The shelter program came to an end. It stopped because the parish questioned the wisdom of its efforts. It debated and concluded that the shelter reinforced addiction and homelessness rather than helped curtail them. So it was replaced by a small covenant-based community—a place to live, struggle and defeat addiction. Now that program thrives. It is home to twenty persons, with a small street-wise staff, a new building and a high rate of success.

Still there are the homeless. They engage and frustrate priest and parishioners on the streets around the church. More come than we could ever see or help. Those who return for appointments are seen. What we offer is respect, a willingness to listen, and the promise to do the best we can to assist. That's not much for those who have so little. But pastoral counseling in any context seldom offers more. Yet, there must be more. It is an issue of justice as well as a matter of service. The city and other churches in the area are all involved.

The other crisis: AIDS. No one sought it, no one could stop it, the community just painfully reacted to it. Pastoral issues are often reactive. We learn what to do as we discover what needs to be done. We learn how to care in the process of caring. This was true of AIDS. Families were hurt and angry. Some disowned their sons. When support was needed the most, many AIDS victims had little. So teams were formed to assist and comfort. They became drivers, sitters, listeners, readers, helpers—compassionate friends. Pastoral care is shaped by the needs it tries to address.

Assistance was given in homes, hospitals and hospices. But much was experienced at worship and within the parish. Though a few provided leadership, the entire congregation was involved. It watched, prayed and agonized while neighbors, Sunday school teachers, choir members, vergers—friends—became increasingly ill. Death came often and grief seemed persistent. All Saints' tarried with those in pain long enough to be honored as a place to come and die.

All Saints' is still being changed. Initiatives bubble up from within, parishioners struggle with personal dilemmas, and the demands of the city are without limit. There is much to do. Programs will be invented to meet needs. All Saints' is being changed because, at various times and ways, parishioners are nourished enough to want to care for others. From within the community, for reasons as varied as its members and relevant to their own lives, people are empowered to serve. Some try to create something new. Others build on past decisions. Still others draw inspiration from the parish's tradition of service. Together with a few others or in concert with a large parish group they contribute to an existing initiative or bring fresh ideas to old urban woes. All Saints' people will change and their programs will too. Caring is like that and so is life. All Saints' is still changing, still vital, because many give thanks for a parish full of people who nourish them with moments of God's presence.

The Rev. George W. Alexander II
Assistant Rector for Pastoral Ministries
All Saints' Episcopal Church
Atlanta, Georgia

CHAPTER VII

Liturgy and Worship

An Invitation into Community

What happens when, on All Saints' Sunday, a family or individual writes Grandma's name on a white cardboard cross and follows the crucifer out of the church to the Memorial Garden, placing the cross among others on the bright green lawn?

Liturgy and worship happen.

What happens when a Florida congregation gathers under the palm trees to cut branches and raise them high as they process into the church singing and shouting Hosanna?

Liturgy and worship happen.

What happens when a congregation in Maine breaks through the frozen earth on the last Sunday after the Epiphany and buries bits and scraps of paper with the word "Alleluia" written on them in the same spot where the crocuses emerge each year as winter gives way to spring and Lent to Easter?

Liturgy and worship happen.

What happens when people and priest gather to break bread and taste wine?

Liturgy and worship happen.

When we do liturgy, God blesses! Our response to God's blessing is worship. The central acts of liturgy are simple and easy to understand. They are a part of our everyday life and meet specific needs.

"Liturgy" comes from a Greek word meaning "public service" or "the people's work"—public work at personal and private cost.

Jesus' liturgy—his life, death and resurrection—is his public service, his personal work at private cost for the salvation of the world. The liturgy of the church is the re-enactment and re-encounter of that liturgy by the church as the Body of Christ.

If liturgy is to become one of the points of entry for people into life in the church and life in Christ, then perhaps the liturgy should be thought of more as a "public service" than a "church service." What does the public need? They need comfort, renewal, celebration, solace, thanksgiving, and intellectual stimulation. They need to acknowledge birth, get married, bury the dead, restore relationships. It is no coincidence that many people approach the church, sometimes for the very first time, at these points in life. Who has not heard about the couple who want to be married in "that cute church"? They come for all the wrong reasons and are often turned away for all the "right" reasons, never to darken the door again. When the church, the Body of Christ, extends herself to the couple through friendship and nurture, the liturgy that will eventually be celebrated on the day of marriage actually begins. Not only is the couple drawn into liturgy, but so are the parents, friends, and guests. This public service becomes the point of contact for God's blessing and the opportunity for worship.

Many congregations have a blessing of animals on St. Francis' Day. One church advertised the service, openly inviting the public to bring their pets. One man who never would have set foot in the church to ask for a blessing for himself came to ask a blessing for his fourteen-year-old German Shepherd. No one present was quite sure what occurred for the dog, but no one could miss the blessing the man received that day. Long before most worshipers begin to develop an understanding of liturgy, they have experienced God's blessing *in* liturgy.

The liturgies of The Book of Common Prayer speak to both the public needs of the people and the worship needs of the faithful. There is a continuing and transforming relationship with God and the world. Liturgy allows the worldly person to maintain a feeling of relevance until the impact of liturgy is able to lead that person into worship. Relevant liturgy embraces apparent needs of God's creation: the world. This is not to say that liturgy is compromised by secularism, but instead, through God's blessing in liturgy, secularism gives way to holiness and the experience of redemption, renewal, or refreshment.

The Book of Common Prayer provides us with the theological and liturgical framework that leads to blessing and worship. There are essential elements for the use of the prayer book for God's work in incorporating new members and renewing current members, thereby reinvigorating the life of the church.

The first is the foundational understanding in Anglicanism that the participants in liturgy are God and the people gathered in God's name—lay people, bishops, priests, and deacons. It is not incidental that the catechism in the prayer book lists the laity as the first order of ministry. The empowerment of the laity takes place through active and significant participation in the liturgy.

This is perhaps most dramatically seen in marriage when the man and woman actually do the liturgy of marriage. The clergy do not marry the couple, they marry each other. Likewise, in the Holy Eucharist, the clergy do not perform it, but celebrate it with the people. Participation in liturgy occurs in a variety of ways. Healthy responses, exchanging the peace, singing the songs, helping a pew mate follow the service, acknowledging our humanity and the humor that arises in most services all add to a sense of participation and belonging. The liturgy is the means by which the church legitimately empowers, upholds and commissions the ministry of the laity, bishops, priests, and deacons.

The second element comes from the very nature of The Book of Common Prayer. The prayer book allows adaptation to any liturgical setting or event that may be encountered. The rubrics of the prayer book give permission to lengthen or shorten certain portions of the liturgy, thus allowing for supplemental liturgies such as commissioning of Christian formation teachers, the welcoming of newcomers, or blessing of animals. An important element in getting people to return for the second visit is the assurance that a time commitment will be honored. The prayer book provides for both order and adaptation.

The prayer book also provides for a variety of worship styles. Examples of the wide range of offerings that may be utilized in the liturgy are clown Eucharists, liturgical dance, skits, and traditional and contemporary music and instrumentation. Through the use of An Order for Celebrating the Holy Eucharist (p. 400), a liturgical service can be designed to fit almost any setting or circumstance imaginable. (This order is not intended for use at the principal Sunday or weekly celebration of the Holy Eucharist.)

Having reflected upon the diverse nature of the liturgy as presented by the prayer book, we come to the third element: the orderly form of the liturgy which is familiar and dependable. People quickly come to know the order of worship and, while they may not have every part memorized, they can absorb the orderliness of the service. There is a structure and sense of order that goes beyond language, so much so that a worshiper can relate to the drama of the liturgy even when visiting another country and experiencing the service in a foreign language. This familiar liturgical encounter allows the person to move into worship and thereby experience solace, strength, pardon and renewal.

Balancing these three aspects of the liturgy with a focus on the needs of the people presents a dynamic situation. By and large, it is pastoral concerns which bring people to church. On any given Sunday those presenting themselves for communion bring with them a great variety of pastoral concerns ranging from celebrations of birth, marriage, and new opportunities, to the sorrows of sickness, death, and losses of every sort and condition. These diverse concerns do not destroy the unity of the foundational purpose of the liturgy. Dom Gregory Dix's classical work on liturgy describes it insightfully:

"At the heart of it all is the eucharistic action, a thing of an absolute simplicity—the taking, blessing, breaking and giving of bread, and the taking, blessing, and giving of a cup of wine and water, as these were first done with their new meaning by a young Jew before and after supper with His friends on the night before He died."*

This single focus of the Eucharist is infectious as the worshiper is drawn into communion with God and all those around the table. In such a liturgical setting people can start turning to one another for support and strength. The liturgical movement re-enacts and re-encounters our Lord's liturgy of salvation.

In a balanced situation where no one person's liturgical preference continuously prevails, all come to share and enjoy the diversity of the liturgy. Special-focus services can be developed which allow groups to move more deeply into liturgical styles that maintain the vigor and dynamism of a diverse community. When this does not occur, both the liturgy and the community will become exclusive and uninviting.

Liturgy done in this inclusive way will help a newcomer feel connected and want to come back.

---

*Dix, Dom Gregory. *The Shape of the Liturgy*. London: A & C Black, 1945. 743f.

Liturgy which includes and celebrates is faithful to Jesus' mandate to love one another. The secular world defines membership with terms of exclusivity; the church encourages new members with words and gestures of inclusiveness. The Lord Jesus Christ in the great liturgy of his life provided a public service to the world once and for all by sharing our human nature, living and dying as one of us to reconcile us to God the Father of all. By this we are blessed and come to worship God.

The Book of Common Prayer continues to offer a unique opportunity to the Episcopal Church to attract new people. It is not to be used as a shield or an obstacle, but instead as a common denominator; not a fence around community, but a gate into fellowship with God and one another.

What happens when the *world* to Christ we bring?

Liturgy and worship, which mysteriously attract, stimulate and invigorate all of God's people.

The Rev. Dr. James H. Cooper, Rector
The Rev. Joan C. Bryan, Associate Rector
The Rev. David R. Wilt, Associate Rector
Christ Church
Ponte Vedra, Florida

CHAPTER VIII

Foundation Stones for Christian Education

While there are hundreds of ways to think and talk about a vibrant Christian education program in the parish, it may be helpful to break down the discussion to a few key points. My experience as a Christian educator in the parish, as well as at diocesan and regional events, has brought me to the sense that there are five foundation stones necessary for a healthy Christian education program. These are: *Intention, Presence, Relationship, Story* and *Joy*. By focusing on each in turn, I hope to open up a new dialogue on the workings of faith formation in a parish setting. It matters very little what curriculum you choose, what subjects you study, what rooms you meet in. What matters most is a vision of what we are trying to accomplish and an on-going dialogue concerning the path that will take us to that end.

Imagine a community of faith in which every member is actively engaged in education, service and worship. Imagine a parish alive with a hunger for the Bible, for the stories of faith, for the wisdom of the catechism, for the food of our Lord at the Eucharist. Imagine what would happen if every young person and adult was a regular participant in the Christian education hour at your parish, and beyond that, active in private study of scripture and readings which open and enhance our understanding of God at work in the world. The very first step in developing healthy and vibrant Christian education in the parish is to allow ourselves to imagine it. In my childhood, my father always used to say, "Amanda, if you don't know where you're going, any road will get you there." Our first task is to determine where we are headed.

What is the end of Christian faith formation? What is the goal? What is our intention?

According to the catechism, the mission of the church is to restore all people to unity with God and each other in Christ. Our intention then must be to work for unity. We must set as our goal the active engagement of all members of the parish, united in faith and fellowship, studying the scripture, sharing concerns, learning together how to live as the true Body of Christ in the world. Our goal is to engage all of God's people in a living relationship with one another and with God.

It sounds like a lofty goal, particularly in this decade, at the turn of the century and the millennium. Increasingly, we live in a culture which is mobile, transitory, and anything but united. Nothing seems solid any more. All truth is presented as relative unless it can be scientifically proven, and the Bible is held up as archaic and mere mythology. In fact, the church is in the unique position of being able to speak to its members with remarkable unity of purpose if we remember that we are a family of faith, a family which does in fact share the basic values of Christian thought, and is committed to remaining in dialogue with one another. We may disagree on the particulars of how to work out our faith and salvation with fear and trembling. But the basic principles of fidelity, loyalty, the sanctity of life, the rich possibility of living our lives together in the common bonds of the incarnate God and the necessity of responding to that incarnation with prayer, worship, study and service, afford us a foundation to stand together in an unsteady world. If we, as Christian educators, hold out the possibility of living in unity with God and with each other in Christ, and if all of our educational programs hold that goal as the chief and primary purpose of our endeavors, then we are off to a good start.

In any Christian education program, our task is not to produce smart Christians who hold all the answers to the difficult questions we face daily, but to struggle together to find God's living word to us, to empower one another to live together, share each other's burdens and joys and stand in unity with one another in the presence of God in Christ. Having unity with God and each other as the goal, we are ready to begin designing programs which will revitalize the church and her members.

Perhaps the most important thing we can bring to any Christian education program in the parish is the ministry of presence. We are people who long for the expert voice. We love to listen to people who know it all on any given subject. So much of our academic training is based on the notion that someone out there knows the answer to the question we are asking, and our task is to find that person or read that book in order to "get it right." But in our parish life and ministry the richest resource we have is one another. Leaders and teachers of Sunday school classes, adult forums, and Wednesday night Bible studies should be encouraged to remember that it is more important that we remain present with one another in the journey of faith than that we provide the "right answer."

So much of what it means to be a Christian boils down to a willingness to stand, to watch and wait with one another, to care for one another by our very presence. Jesus said he would send his Holy Spirit to live and move in us so that we would not be without comfort. In the training of leaders and teachers, not enough is said about the ministry of presence. It is all right for us to admit our ignorance, to ask hard questions, even to decide that we disagree on the meaning of a certain scripture passage or teachings in the catechism, as long as we remain present to one another.

Jesus is our model. No matter how many questions his disciples asked, no matter how foolish or stubborn they became, even when they didn't understand a word he was saying, he remained with them. Jesus is our model for an education based on presence. By the indwelling power of the Christ and his Holy Spirit we can remain with one another, remain present to one another, and by doing so, build relationships with one another.

A vibrant Christian education program is built on relationships. Leaders and participants must come into relationship with one another. The didactic model, one lecturer and a room full of note-takers, is the least effective way to establish true intimacy. At the end of an hour lecture, individuals in the group may know a few more facts, but they will not know each other or the leader. Christian education requires that we both know and be known by one another. Teams of leaders will find they work better together in the classroom if they have spent time together in their homes. Small dinner parties for Sunday school teachers held every other month in the homes of parishioners will do more to enliven your Sunday school programs than a new curriculum, or a new box of markers and a bulletin board. Small groups struggling over the meaning of a prayer in our celebrations of the Eucharist, invitations to pray for one another daily between Sunday or Wednesday night meetings, and time allowed for members of any group to ask their questions and share their insights, to tell one another the story of their own faith journey, and to listen closely to the struggles and concerns of others—all are essential to a healthy education program.

This is true at every level of Christian education.

Even the youngest members of a parish will benefit from allowing time to build relationships. Ask a three or four-year-old, "What would you like to pray about today?" The answer will be much the same as the answer of a seventy-five-year-old church veteran: safety, health, happiness, provision for our needs. The words we choose may change depending on our age, but as we share our lives with one another, we find our common bonds, the ground for the unity which is at the heart of our intention. Activities where individuals are engaged in questions of faith, service work, and simple participation in some kind of show-and-tell—this is my life, these are my blessings and burdens—make it possible for us to find the living Christ in one another. It is in relationship with one another that we can begin to find the truth.

Having said that, it would be naive to maintain that only relationships and presence are necessary for a healthy Christian education program. There is more to it than simply talking to one another, or working on some project for the benefit of others. We must also incorporate a time for listening to and telling the Story. We must learn ways to let our lives be informed by scripture. For many of us the Bible story, from beginning to end, is a mystery. We have heard it only in snippets through our lectionary readings. We are not familiar with the rhythm and cadence of the whole of the story, and in fact we are ignorant of so many of the stories, and unwilling even to admit our ignorance. Christian education, if it is to be vibrant and true to its mission, will employ scripture as story. Scripture holds the true stories of God's action in history and humankind's struggle to respond to God's love. We can never over-estimate the importance of the Bible.

In working with young people and with adults, I have found that one of the most effective ways for entering into stories of faith is through the back door. I encourage Christian educators to know the stories, especially those found in the gospels. Knowing them, we can begin to see our lives in a new light. When my own son, William, is asked to help search for a lost diamond in the check-out line in the grocery store, I can recognize his experience as akin to the parable of the Lost Coin, or the Pearl of Great Price. I can tell the story of William at the grocery store first, engaging the group in a true story from my life, and then, coming in the back door, point them to the stories Jesus told about sacrificing oneself and one's possessions in order to find the kingdom of God. If we know the stories, we can begin to see that our own lives are often parables of the kingdom.

As we learn to tell the stories, acting them out in skits, memorizing certain key verses to help us remember the whole story, sharing not only the written word of God with one another, but also our own living-the-gospel stories, we will open up the possibility of being alive and awake to God's action in ways which will continually empower us to be obedient and faithful.

While it is important that we be informed on matters of justice and peace, politics and political action, we must ground all our discussions in the light of the gospels and the whole of scripture. This is only possible if regular and rigorous Bible study is at the center of Christian education. We need to know the stories. The more we know what is written in the Bible, and tell one another the stories of our own daily lives, the greater the possibility our people will find consolation and strength in a difficult and secular world.

Finally, there must be a certain joy in all we do. Joy is one of the fruits of the Holy Spirit. Christian education programs need not be somber and earnest all the time. Humor and laughter are healers. We come to church on Sunday mornings to worship, to celebrate, to have a joyful party in the house of God. Sunday school classrooms should be places where joy reigns, laughter and giggling are commonplace. The world is serious enough. God has invited us to the banquet; we come with party clothes and plain clothes to celebrate the mysteries of faith.

What does it mean to hold our intention, presence, relationship, story and joy as the cornerstones of Christian education? In my experience it boils down to nurturing one another in faith. It means that instead of holding earnest and "meaningful" meetings to plan the next adult series or the next five weeks of a Sunday school class, we welcome one another into joy. As we design our programs, we allow for didactics at every level, but also make room for the sharing of our own insights and concerns. We celebrate the indwelling Christ in each other by listening to one another. There may be more information about Christ in his church in a Polaroid snapshot of young people laughing together in their classroom than in all the earnest discussion of the meaning of the sacraments we can muster. A vibrant

Christian education program balances study with laughter, prayer with listening to one another, service with a desire to find God in solitude. All these things and more make up the richness of our life together, and as we structure programs which allow for all our experience to come into play, into questions, into celebration, we honor the Christ in one another.

Much has been said about the flight to certainty, that trend in mainstream denominations to a literal interpretation of scripture, hard and fast rules of conduct, and sturdy definitions of sin and obedience. These denominations are growing by leaps and bounds. Nevertheless, in the community of faith which I imagine, it is never a flight into certainty which beckons to me; it is a rush into relationships, presence, stories and joy. We open the possibility of living in unity with God and one another in Christ when we structure programs which allow people time and space to love one another—children and adults, little ones and teenagers—singing, working side by side, celebrating the diversity of our experience, raking leaves, engaging in service projects with the poor, the hungry, the disenfranchised, carrying in covered dishes for evening study groups, learning of the rich heritage of our Gospel stories and the history of our faith tradition, and finally kneeling together at the rail to receive the precious body and blood of our Lord. Those moments when we are sharing with one another the best and worst parts of our days and weeks and years—telling one another our life stories, working side by side, laughing, crying, studying, celebrating, all the while learning the foundations of our faith—are the moments when we experience the true incarnation of God in our midst.

Amanda Millay Hughes,
lecturer in Christian education,
communicant,
St. Philip's Episcopal Church
Durham, North Carolina

Building Up the Church

CHAPTER IX

Marks of Vitality in Adult Education

From my experience, a healthy, growing congregation is one deeply committed to offering a full range of adult education. The congregation has a clear vision and a high priority for adult education. I offer six marks of vitality in adult education along with examples of where and how adult education is working.

1. **A Story.** A story from the Old Testament gives me a symbol of my ministry as a church educator. Pharaoh decided to weaken the Hebrew people by killing off all the infant males. Moses' mother hid her infant son along the banks of the Nile. When Pharaoh's daughter rescued the infant, Moses' mother offered herself as the nanny for the child. My imagination moves me beyond the text. I picture Moses' mother whispering the stories of the Hebrews into the ears of her son as she raised him under the nose of Pharaoh. Pharaoh's story was not to guide Moses as he grew up. Moses had an alternative story

that shaped his consciousness (Exodus 2:1-10 and 3:1-22).

2. **A Vision.** Years later Moses stood before the burning bush and heard the voice of God calling him to lead the Hebrew people out of slavery and into the promised land. God spoke as ". . . the God of your father, the God of Abraham, the God of Isaac and the God of Jacob" (Exodus 3:6). Because Moses knew the story of his people, he knew he was a Hebrew and not an Egyptian. Because he knew the story, he could respond to God's call. Because he knew the story, he had a sense of where God was leading the people. Moses had an alternative story that gave him an alternative vision and an alternative ethic. He saw his whole life through the lens of that narrative.

Today we have a renewed appreciation for the importance of narrative in the church. Without a memory growing out of the story, we have no sense of vision and no understanding of sacred calling to be God's people in the world today.

3. **A Process.** The cathechumenal process that has roots in ancient church practice has been reintroduced partly because it provides a way of living into the biblical story. The process assumes that the first step in conversion leading to adult baptism, confirmation, reaffirmation and reception is to tell the church's story. Participants respond with their own stories of encounters with God. The second stage of the process invites participants to place their personal stories into dialogue with the church's story. Conversion and empowerment for ministry come as the church's story becomes the lens through which

Building Up the Church

individuals begin to perceive their lives. We look back to our historic roots to discover models for education today.

4. **A language and practice of baptismal transformation.** *Called to Teach and Learn: A Cathechetical Guide for the Episcopal Church* is an official document of the Episcopal Church produced by the Ministry with Young People's Cluster at the Episcopal Church Center. A major emphasis in this guide is the shift from the language and practice of education to the language and practice of catechesis: "The language of Christian education . . . has traditionally been associated with schooling, knowledge about intellectual content, and instructional techniques . . . Catechetics, on the other hand, has been concerned with aiding individuals and communities in acquiring and deepening the Christian life of faith." Catechesis ". . . includes all the means by which we prepare new Christians for baptism, and aid all the baptized to live into their baptism and become who they already are—Christians—but in ever deeper and fuller ways." The catechumenal process is one important part of this life-changing approach. Using the theories of catechesis rather than education is a constant reminder that what we offer in our congregations is not adult courses in Bible appreciation, but rather a combination of content and experience that move people to conversion and commitment.

5. **A Calendar.** The church's calendar of seasons, holy days and commemorations tells the Christian story over the course of the year. The calendar is a built-in catechetical tool, for it evolved as a dynamic way of preparing people for their baptism as well as

a way of reflecting on the meaning of baptism for the rest of their lives. Adult catechesis based on the lectionary and congregational worship is a way of forming and transforming a people. This is the goal of catechesis. Don't be concerned about people *knowing* more. Rather be concerned that people are *seeing* more. Enable people to see through the lens of the Gospel.

6. **A priority.** Keeping the story of Moses' call to leadership in mind, adult catechesis must be a top priority in the life of the congregation. Adult catechesis is not simply a case of teaching about our relationship with God. It is an invitation to stand before the burning bush and be able to identify the God who calls us. The role of adult catechesis is to equip the congregation with a memory that informs a vision and empowers the church to act in the present. Martin Luther King Jr. proclaimed a dream driven by the memory of the Exodus. The memory and the vision moved the people to action and gave focus to their witness for justice.

With the crucial importance of adult catechesis in mind, I offer some hopeful signs that give me encouragement as a church educator today.

First, there is a growing hunger for spiritual roots. "Spirituality" is no longer a word for the church alone. Check the book and magazine displays at the airport, local supermarket and bookstore. This interest is a call for renewal in the church. Adult catechesis becomes the companion on the seeker's way.

In Dialogue with Scripture: An Episcopal Guide to Studying the Bible is an important resource available from parish services associated with the Episcopal Church Center. The launching of the first edition included a major Bible study conference several years ago. Over two hundred people came for five days of intensive training in Bible teaching and study skills. Deputies to General Convention frame their day with scripture dialogue, and the House of Bishops spends time each day with the Word as well as with the agenda. Serious dialogue with scripture sets the tone for meetings in congregations, dioceses and national church events.

In the Diocese of Pennsylvania over a hundred church teachers from across the diocese gather for an evening of training and preparation for their work as teachers in the congregations of the diocese. Two other major weekend events are scheduled for the fall.

A rector of a parish begins each parish meeting with twenty minutes of adult education using easily read Forward Movement or Scriptographic booklets.

A commitment to serious study brings persons together in a four-year weekly study of theology. Other adult education programs call for a similar commitment to study. When adults perceive a clear benefit they become involved in committed study.

The catechumenal process mentioned above is taking root in the church. Lives are being changed with extensive exposure to word and sacrament. Ministry is a response to the baptismal covenant rather than a synonym for ordination. Lutherans and Episcopalians share national training events for catechists, and United Methodists are adapting the ancient process.

Dialogue on controversial theological and social questions has become a part of the church's life. Though seen as a burdensome task for some, others note that the dialogue has launched an involvement in important issues facing the church and society today.

The Baptismal Covenant from the baptismal rite in The Book of Common Prayer is influencing the way the church sees ministry. The five questions including "will you seek and serve Christ in all persons . . . strive for justice and peace among all people . . ." have provided a way of evaluating congregational life. It is often the rites of the prayer book that set the pace of church life.

Last summer some 1,400 young people participated in a national Episcopal Youth Event. At least some of tomorrow's young adults will expect an engagement with God's word unfolding in scripture, tradition, and the exciting happenings of the moment.

The coordinator of Children's Ministries at the Episcopal Church Center reports that adults involved with children find themselves drawn into searching for God with other adults as their ministry with children awakens their own needs and questions. Children minister to adults as they witness to the wonder of discovering God, and it is catching!

All Saints', Pasadena, California, offers a rector's study every Sunday that draws from 200 to 300 persons. Major speakers from outside the parish as well as parish leaders address the forum on a variety of social and theological issues. St. Michael and All Angels in Dallas, Texas, averages 350 to 400 adults participating in education on Sunday morning, 200 doing Bible study during the week and another 400 involved in courses and special adult education. Spirituality, self-discovery, prayer, Bible study, and parenting skills draw the most interest. A wide variety of courses and workshops is offered. Though these are large parishes, it is the long-term commitment to offer excellence in adult education rather than size that determines the vitality of the process of adult catechesis. Video, audio tapes and print resources provide the same opportunity for exploration of ideas and issues that is available to the larger congregations.

Flexibility is a hallmark of successful adult education programs in today's church. Internet courses, teleconferencing programs, individual study with a mentor, and audio or visual tape programs are ways of involving persons in study. A new publishing and training organization offers education designs on computer disk so that dioceses and congregations can shape the education or training process to fit their specific needs. Rather than publishing printed texts and providing expert teachers and trainers, the goal is to help create learning communities.

The Episcopal-Lutheran Concordat points to adult education opportunities growing out of this important breakthrough in ecumenical relations. Episcopalians and Lutherans seek a clearer picture of who we are as separate bodies, and who we can become in a closer relationship.

These are but a few areas where the church is showing a new vitality in the face of tremendous changes that propel us into the next century.

The writer of the Letter to the Ephesians saw the need for ". . . building up the body of Christ, until all of us come to the unity of the faith and of the knowledge of the Son of God, to maturity, to the measure of the full stature of Christ" (Ephesians 4:12-13). That concern still frames the vision for the church today. We have a sacred calling—a vocation—to break open the Word of God.

The Rev. Joseph P. Russell,
member of the Standing
Liturgical Commission,
former Assistant to the Bishop
of Ohio for Christian Education

CHAPTER X

Lowering the Bar

The title for this chapter comes from my friend, Charles Bennison, Bishop of Pennsylvania. In a large study of parishes that were healthy and growing, he observed that those churches were "upping the ante" in terms of people's commitment to Christ (more substantial Bible study, for example), and "lowering the bar" in terms of finding ways to help people to become more a part of the community. This chapter is about lowering the bar.

If you are reading this book, there is a good chance that going to or working in the church is something that is an integral part of your life. For many people, however, church is something unfamiliar, unusual and mysterious. In order to be helpful and empathize with newcomers, sensitivity to this point of view is needed, not only in the way you greet people at your worship service, but at other times when they reach out to you.

In my experience there are three entry or re-entry points in people's lives—special times: their weddings, the birth of children, and the death of loved ones. We need to be very careful at these crucial times. To be careful means to be compassionate and not overly dogmatic, to listen rather than to tell, and to remember how tentative and uncertain you were when you went someplace where you didn't know your way around.

This is not merely a familiar call for inclusivity. This is a call for us to share our rites. This is our chance to make the church more open and accessible. To illustrate my point, I offer three stories of lost chances for outreach and evangelism through our rites.

At a recent gathering of Episcopal clergy I ran into a priest who had been retired for about ten years. The topic of how well the church retains its children as adults came up. "Well, I can tell you, the church didn't lose my son, they drove him away," said the retired priest. I asked him to explain. His son had called his local Episcopal parish and inquired about having a home baptism. The clergyperson on the line indignantly told him in a condescending way, "We don't do home baptisms in the Episcopal Church anymore." The priest's son uttered a "Gee, thanks" and hung up the phone. "Well that's it," he declared to his wife and first-born baby, "we'll never darken those doors again." The priest telling me the story gave a wistful sigh and asked, "What is happening to our church?"

Since the adoption of the 1979 prayer book, virtually all clergy have tried to move baptisms from the home into the main worship life of the church. This article is not arguing that the policy should change. But for many, baptisms are not baptisms unless they are at home. Quite a few people haven't set foot in church since 1979 and they need sensitive pastoral care more than they need a lesson on church doctrine. This is a teaching opportunity.

A friend called me the other day. He asked if I would perform his marriage ceremony at the church where I worked. I assured him that I would be happy to officiate. Then I asked why he wasn't going to be married in his hometown parish where he had been acolyte and youth group member. "It's against church policy," he said in a mock official voice. He told me that the parish had instituted a new policy stating that you could be married there only if you were the bride and only if your parents had been members in good standing (read: pledging member) for more than five years.

"Ouch," I exclaimed, "I've never heard of a policy that restrictive." "Restrictive and reverse sexist," muttered my friend. "I should sue them for discriminating against men." I tried to assuage his anger by saying that I thought there must have been a lot of demand to celebrate weddings in that parish church. "Sure, but my family has been a part of the church for 40 years; my grandparents are still members." He went on to explain that his bride, a child of a military family, was never in one place long enough to develop a parish home and so was open to being married in the groom's church. "I used to think it was my church," said my friend. I did the wedding, but three generations of loyal members of the other church were deeply saddened.

None of us wants the church to be used like a

movie set for an event. I have had calls from people who saw their conversation with me to be of the same importance as the chat they had with the caterer a moment before. However, I think that in our zeal to protect the church most churches have gone overboard in ultra-restrictive marriage policies. If you are not willing to leave the door of opportunity open a crack, then how are you going to let the Holy Spirit in to do good works? A more open policy toward marriages could also give you many hours with the couple to show that yours is a welcoming community. If you are bemoaning the absence of a vital young adults ministry in your parish, look at your wedding policy.

Geoffrey Hoare, rector of St. Paul's in Alexandria, Virginia, has a very enlightened approach to this difficult dilemma. St. Paul's is a gorgeous, spacious church in the heart of Old Town Alexandria, attractive to people planning weddings. After performing 45 weddings his first year there (virtually for every single couple that asked him) Geoffrey decided that enough was enough and he cut way back. Then he realized that there were great outreach and evangelism opportunities being lost. He developed a new policy. Now he agrees to do one "newcomer" wedding a month. In this way the door is not shut to people returning to the church, and Geoffrey is not spinning his wheels doing numerous weddings for people who may never return.

Another friend told me a story that came as a big surprise. He had been a priest associate at a west coast parish for many years. He had filled in for the rector many times for midweek services, funerals and an occasional Sunday. One day the wife of an inactive parishioner died and the widower called my friend and asked if he would do the service at the church. The priest associate said that he was almost positive it would be OK, but he would call to make sure. The rector was not in, so my friend left a comprehensive message on voice mail. The next day there was a letter in my friend's mail box and, to his great surprise, the rector said no. He cited a need to serve the existing parish first and said how hard it was to help those with no connection to the parish.

My friend reminded me that the couple had been married in the parish some fifty years ago. I expressed my sadness and surprise. As a rector, I know how easy it would be for me to let a priest associate conduct a funeral service at the church where I work. It struck me as a remarkable slight to the priest associate as well as to the man who had just lost his wife.

How many times have we, clergy or lay person, bumped into people who say to us, "Oh, I ran into you at the funeral in your church last month"? Funerals are a time of grieving, not just for the parish but for the community at large. When you turn down the funeral, you turn down the community. In my experience funerals, like weddings and baptisms, are an opportunity for healing. A friend who is a priest in southeast USA received a call from a woman who sounded very business-like. She said, "I'll make no bones about it, I didn't like your predecessor and so I haven't been in church in eight years, but my husband has died and I want to have a funeral service for him." My friend was gracious and welcoming and handled the arrangements as though the person had been in the church for years. The woman and her children have returned to the church and are very active.

The woman's voice on my phone was tearful. Not unusual in the life of a parish priest. But what made this call different was that she called me by my first name. "Rob, can you baptize my daughter?" she asked emotionally. "Sure," I said, "who is this?" She told me that she was the wife of my wife's good friend. Although we had met just once, I told her that I remembered her and that I would be happy to baptize her daughter. I asked why she wouldn't be going to her local parish for the baptism. She sobbed. "The rector told me that he was trying to cut down on baptisms," she cried into the phone.

"Cutting down on baptisms," I thought, "now there is something that never came to my mind." I suspected that that was what the woman had heard, but I was sure that was not what the rector meant. "Are you sure that is what he said?" I asked. "Well, he said that there were too many baptisms on too many Sundays and he was instituting a policy of only doing baptisms on the five major feast days. He said it in a really snippy way." I told her that was not a policy that I would ever fully embrace but that some consider it liturgically and historically appropriate.

"But," she gasped, "my husband's grandfather can only get to our area in July since he has been so ill." There are no major feast days in July. I told her that I would be happy to do the baptism in July but I encouraged her to reconnect with her rector. "Are you kidding," she said, "we'll never go back there. My husband is adamant." As I wrote the baptismal date in my daytimer, I worried about a four-generation church relationship going sour due either to a bad policy or some real miscommunication.

Once again, a chance for education and outreach was lost due to a misunderstanding. This family was tearful, not just because the baptism wouldn't be in their family church, but because their fifty-year relationship with the parish seemed to be going up in smoke. How hard will it be for this family to reconnect with the parish again?

Avid students of the 1979 prayer book will no doubt be pointing to the rubric on page 312: "Holy Baptism is especially appropriate at the Easter Vigil, on the Day of Pentecost, on All Saints' Day or the Sunday after All Saints' Day, and on the Feast of the Baptism of our Lord . . . It is recommended that, as far as possible, Baptisms be reserved for these occasions or when a bishop is present." Marion Hatchett, writing in his commentary on the prayer book* observes that these limitations were put in place by the Council of Toledo in 398 as a way for deacons to baptize legally since there weren't enough priests or bishops—hardly the condition now. This is a rubric that can be too rigidly understood.

---

* Hatchett, Marion J., *Commentary on the American Prayer Book*, Harper & Row, San Francisco, 1980.

How can we be protectors of the faith and at the same time be open to people in their faith journeys? The answer lies in prayerful deliberation on how we share our rites. Jesus often shocked his followers when he defied convention and invited outsiders to break bread with him. Should we do less?

The Rev. Robert M. Ross, Rector
St. Peter's Church
Osterville, Massachusetts

CHAPTER XI

Stewardship

Henry Probasco, who gave the City of Cincinnati the fountain that creates Fountain Square, completely absorbed my thoughts as I walked past the beggar at the corner of Walnut and Fifth streets, pretending not to see him. His back was up against a wall; he sat facing the fountain.

My walks through Fountain Square are infrequent, but I knew I had seen this man before, his need so obvious—crippled, ill-clad, dirty, hat outstretched—and tried not to notice him. I did see the older man, ahead of me, walking just slowly enough to block my view of the beggar. I strode ahead, passed them both and rounded the corner onto Walnut.

Retired, wearing a hat, red shirt, dark blue trousers and black shoes, the older man reached his right hand around to his hip pocket. I knew exactly what was happening. Imagining that he remembered Sunday's sermon and the passage, "Inasmuch as you have done it unto one of the least of these. . . ," I became uncomfortable and walked faster, but not too fast for three quick backward glances. Out came the wallet. He stopped, dead in his tracks, carefully counted his money, turned back to the beggar and give him a bill.

And what did I do? What else could I do? I re-crossed the street and did the same.

There is one reason, and only one reason, why the church exists—to proclaim Jesus Christ, crucified and resurrected, until he comes again. Once we have been baptized, our lives are defined by this reality. It claims us, and we live our lives to express it.

But too often—most of the time—we are reluctant to become involved. Involvement means we have to offer ourselves, go out of our way. Sometimes secretly, sometimes openly and hungrily, we crave what the Lord Christ offers. But much of the time we'll do anything, find any excuse, walk away, wall ourselves off from the Lord Christ. We'd rather avoid what his presence demands. But again and again, there he is, sitting on the corner. We'll only come to know him when we give of our selves.

A steward is willing to know the Lord by giving. All that we have and all that we are is God's gift. The gift is given to the steward with the confidence that we will use it well, use it to proclaim Jesus Christ, crucified and resurrected, until he comes again. The steward is an expression of God's presence.

God came, God dwelt, God lived and died and was raised again in the midst of the stuff of our life. God's presence is real and substantial—incarnate. Those who live out the expression of the Christian faith are involved in the real stuff of life, which includes money.

Wealth is an aspect of the image of God reflected

in our human nature. Wealth has many expressions, but money is first and foremost in the United States. Stewardship is focused in the use, the giving and receiving, of money.

The parish church proclaims Christ through the gathering of God's people to receive the sacraments, to hear the Word, to share God's love in the world. The parish preaches Jesus Christ through the presence and contribution of stewards, whose work of stewardship combines four elements.

Vision

"Where there is no vision, the people perish" (Proverbs 29:18). Before all else there is vision, simply articulated, well understood.

Our vision is clear: to proclaim Jesus Christ, crucified and resurrected, until he comes again. Stewardship is proclaiming that vision and inviting others to share in it. Stewardship is implementing this vision in meaningful and decisive ways . . .

Jack is a single-minded man. His life has always been full: three businesses, two families, a series of houses, four major moves. Jack has many friends, always has, and they know him as genial, kind and always on the go, thinking about others and, mostly, what he can do for them. It's clear-cut, obvious. Jack is a person of whom it is often said: "What you see is what you get."

Anytime you listen to Jack—even for three or four minutes—you'll discover how it happened. While Jack was playing tackle on the state university championship football team, he decided the time had come to make some decisions. The first one was to devote his life to the Lord. He realized that football was only a game and the stakes in life were far higher. But there were rules, a goal, and events had consequences. It was all very clear. No question about it.

From that day forward, life had a plan, and the plan centered in the Lord. It provided a framework for family and business, the way he spent his spare time and allocated their income. He was the Lord's, centered his life in the Lord and his intention to bring other persons to him. It was all very clear. Sharing the vision.

Incarnation

The Christian faith rests upon the Incarnation. Our vision is born from the fact that God came, God cared, God died, God was raised from the dead to breathe life into each one of us. The steward embodies the vision.

The presence of Christ lives and breathes in each of us. Here on this earth, God's work surely is our own. Our task is to embody the vision. Stewardship, born of vision, calls us forth to invest ourselves in our Lord's great commission, "Go ye into all the world to preach the gospel." We do so aware that our strength, our future, our mission are the sum total of all of our resources: spiritual, personal, financial . . .

Ed lived to be 97. His vision was clouded; he walked and thought more slowly, but he was very much himself. We'd been friends for more than thirty years, first meeting just after he'd finished his work to defeat massive resistance in the Commonwealth of Virginia to racial integration.

Our friendship did include my presence on a Monday morning as the Supreme Court sat before us, high and lifted up. Solicitor General Cox, dressed in morning coat and striped pants, stood before them, as Ed argued, and won, for the plaintiffs in the 1965, 6-3, one-man-one-vote decision. Years later I commented that after *Brown vs. the Board of Education* (1954) this was the most important Supreme Court decision of our time. Ed replied, "I think you're right."

Near the end of Ed's life, he and I again sat and talked one afternoon, and I asked him why he had become a lawyer. It was not for financial gain. Was it the love of argument, or a passionate interest in the law?

"One reason and one reason only. It gave me a platform, a place, a reason to pursue peace and justice. To make a difference in the world."

That was exactly what he did.

Intentionality

God's grace is all-sufficient, but the channel for that grace is the intention we bring to our tasks. Events, persons and resources coalesce when planning and intentionality bring persons and program and promise together. Stewardship is the concerted effort to enable vision to create our future.

Nowhere is this more clear than when it comes to financial support. Giving in the church is a responsive activity. The gift that is given and received must be specifically requested—*asked for with intentionality*—to provide form and substance for the vision . . .

He was sick and tired of hearing people say, "I'll do anything for you, absolutely anything, except help you raise money." If you believed in what you were doing, it was all very simple. What you did was go and sit down with one person at a time and tell the story, tell it fully and as powerfully as you were able. And then you asked that person for a specific gift to help the story continue. You asked for support. You asked for money. He'd done it a hundred times—two hundred. And not once, not once, had anyone ever said "no."

The money for which he asked was going to be given to someone and for some purpose. He was asking a fellow human being to join him in building up the body of Christ, helping them understand that there is one reason why the church exists—to proclaim Jesus Christ, crucified and resurrected, until he comes again.

Belonging

Stewardship is about belonging, the opportunity for many different persons to claim ownership of the common work that reflects who they are and what they believe. Once we belong, we give. We want to give to what we value. We give of ourselves and our worth, because we belong, because we have been empowered . . .

Warren and Nellie Cobb lived at the end of a dirt

road, well outside of town. Warren was blind, had been for forty years, ever since the battery acid dropped in his face at work in the auto repair shop, just before he finished at MIT. Since then, he'd held several jobs, good ones, before the days when there was understanding about disability. Warren read Braille books, voraciously—theology was his special interest—listened to baseball on the radio, debated endlessly with the neighbors, and he prayed.

He and Nellie boarded retarded adults. The compensation from the state wasn't much—$1200 a year—but it was enough to get by on. They were in church whenever they got a ride into town. Every month Warren sent the parish a letter, full of strikeovers and all kinds of news. He always enclosed $2 in new bills.

Deep in our hearts we know. We know we are not our own, but His, yet still we run and dodge—until we are grasped by the **Vision** made full and real by the **Incarnation** that offers us **Intentionality** and the full reality of **Belonging**. Then there will be no choice but to give ourselves to Him. That choice is ours today.

The Rev. Edward S. Gleason,
Editor of Forward Movement Publications,
former Director of Development,
Virginia Theological Seminary

CHAPTER XII

Discernment

Give them an inquiring and discerning heart . . .

—Prayer for the Newly Baptized,
The Book of Common Prayer

Discernment: the work of trying to know the mind of God. It is a preposterous undertaking, on the face of it; but it is one in which God's people have always been absorbed, apparently because God wants it that way. All the prophets talked back, questioning their call, insisting on clarification. The psalmists confronted God with their frustrations and sufferings, and demanded an explanation. Even Jesus drew his disciples into defining who exactly he was supposed to be, and met his death with the urgent question of Psalm 22: "My God, my God, why have you forsaken me?" We may never get it quite right, but faithfulness requires us to try.

The Anglican tradition does not ask faithful people to shut up and knuckle under. It rejects the image of a God who surrounds us with rigid rules and has vengeance ready when we break them. It begins with a God who gives us freedom and a vigorous challenge to live our lives with passion and joy. Prohibitions give way to the lively summons of the gospel: to ask, seek, knock, love, serve, feed, tend, bless, forgive.

What this might mean for us in any particular situation is hardly ever spelled out. Instead, we are given pictures of people doing absurd things: a half-crazy farmer who scatters precious seed on barren ground; a father who runs down the road to welcome his wandering son; a compulsive housewife who crawls around searching for a lost coin and gives a party when she finds it; and especially a man who ruins his reputation by hanging out with outcasts, and dies asking forgiveness for his executioners. It's as if God had given us an immense present, all in pieces, with no instructions, only a mischievous invitation: "*You* figure it out!" And with that, the images of various apostles, in conditions that range from total confusion to outrageous, burning certainty.

Our discernment begins with this God whose love of us is without limits and beyond the calculations of ordinary human justice. With such a God cheering us on, we can go ahead with confidence, even knowing that we are sure to get it wrong much of the time. The guiding principle is not perfection but forgiveness, given again and again.

Discernment in community

Discernment is not work that we do alone. As our first systematic theologian, Richard Hooker, noted four centuries ago, our meaning-making rests on a "three-legged stool," and each leg consists of the insights of many seekers. Scripture is the first leg, the starting point, the record of God's long love affair with the human race, God's irrepressible Word speaking to us through a marvelous crowd of flawed and inspired witnesses. Tradition is the second leg, and brings us the accumulated understanding and practice of many centuries. "Right reason," the third leg, introduces the fresh revelations of God made to us through our present experience, but always connected to (though sometimes in tension with) a community of faith. And then around to scripture again, to encounter God's Word still more deeply.

There is no end to this work. The three legs are always getting out of balance, becoming idols, as everything can if it is not God. Reliance on scripture becomes biblical literalism, lines taken out of context and made into bludgeons, creative Word frozen into paralyzing dogma. Tradition dries out, becomes "the way we've always done it," a barricade against the Holy Spirit. "Right reason" blurs into faddishness and self-justification, eternal verities bent to current fashion. So we have to go around again, scripture and tradition and right reason, as God keeps making all things new and we have to keep on wondering what God has in mind this time.

It can be an unnerving process—and is, in fact, to many lifelong churchpeople, who long for comfort and peace. They come to church hoping to find a truth they can hold onto, once and for all. As old assumptions are called into question and old certainties shaken, the very essence of the faith can

Building Up the Church

seem to be in jeopardy. Especially in a time when hardly anything is trustworthy, a church that is willing to test its own beliefs and practices can seem to be a church that has lost its soul. People get scared, and frightened people get angry, and decorum is overwhelmed by polarization, name-calling, demonizing, threats, and sometimes permanent division.

For Episcopalians, what works against the fear is first of all our worship, our common prayer. Our prayer book does change, but very slowly. It conserves the words and rhythms and gestures of many centuries of worshipers, and draws our jittery minds into a solemn, lovely dance. It has intractable opponents moving together, saying things that any one of them may not believe completely at any one time, but that all of them pronounce in unison. It instructs us to wish God's incomprehensible peace to neighbors we can't comprehend and maybe can't stand. It gathers us around a table with people we may not know and might never choose, and tells us that we are all loved without reservation, and furthermore, essential to one another.

The Holy Eucharist, the visible symbol of the invisible body of Christ, is the basis for our discernment. This sacrament is our weekly reminder of what we have many reasons to forget: every single one of us is precious, welcome and redeemed. Discernment starts with this divine guarantee that there is infinite treasure to be found among us. It promises wonderful surprises when we use not just our logical heads but our inquiring and discerning hearts. It places our safety not in right answers but in Christ's free gift of grace.

The work of discernment is grounded in the joy of that gift. It removes any excuse for getting paralyzed by our own confusion, or our fear of getting it wrong. We *will* get it wrong sometimes, and some of our errors will be huge. But this family table is for strength, not just solace; for renewal, along with the pardon. This food is nourishment for action.

Discernment for the congregation

So what do we do now? Figuring that out is a Christian congregation's ongoing work. Those endless, slogging committee meetings take on new life when you imagine that every individual present bears Christ's image, and might speak with Christ's voice any minute now. Intellectual battles don't make much sense when everybody has a part of the truth, and the fun is in discovering what part each person knows. Squabbling yields to attentive listening. Old combative habits can be broken by starting with prayer, stopping for prayer, and ending with prayer, so there's room for God to talk.

This process is not efficient. Sometimes we wish that Jesus had been a little more specific in his instructions; but sometimes his instructions are all too clear. "Take no thought for tomorrow," he says blithely. "Consider the lilies of the field." "Do not store up for yourselves treasures on earth." Clear and, for most of us, completely unrealistic.

It's not an accident that Jesus talked about money so much. The subject of money absorbs our most incoherent passions, and turns budget meetings into holy wars. Often the chief casualty is the treasurer, whose mandate is to keep us solvent and assure our financial future. Hardheaded economics, designed for a precarious world, run smack into the extravagant economy of the kingdom.

We know there's a difference; we know that in order to live on this earth we have to be practical, wise as serpents. Dumb idealists aren't of much use, even in churches. But always the kingdom is our context, the unseen reality that flashes dimly through the dark mirror now and then. It tells us that we are not a business but something else, and that the God who makes us something else is worth risking everything for, even our lives. Vestries used to be able to think of themselves as nuts-and-bolts people and leave the spiritual stuff to the clergy. Gradually we are learning that our incarnational faith sees the nuts-and-bolts stuff as raw material for the kingdom, and vestries are daring to imagine that they might be spiritual leaders too. But how do we know when it is not just the annual budget but the kingdom itself that is at stake?

Discernment in moral decisions

Discernment is urgently needed in the matter of moral teachings as well. Once we thought we knew what Christian morality was, and if we sinned, we knew that too. Now many of us seem to know many different and mutually exclusive things; and some of the most certain rules are cast as prejudice and hardness of heart.

This struggle is particularly evident in the area of sexual practices, where we react out of deep and often unconscious convictions and fight to protect what may seem to be the fundamental structures of our lives. Scriptural sources are revisited and challenged by everyone from biblical scholars to anthropologists as mistranslations or cultural bias. We are disturbed by a Savior who violated society's rules by eating with outcasts, and welcomed those whom others shunned as unclean—but who also had no use for permissiveness: "Go and sin no more." And in our midst are newly visible witnesses who teach the church that love and commitment and fidelity and sacrifice are not confined to old forms, and raise difficult questions about the link between our bodies and our souls.

In nearly every area of our corporate life, new voices challenge our certainties, and teach us humility. People of different races and cultures and classes confront Anglican evangelism with evidence of how narrowly "English" some of our most cherished traditions are, and gradually we make room for other expressions of holiness. For those who have clung to the church as a bastion of security, that can be terrifying. But again, what works against the fear is our wonder at this body of Christ, which is turning out to be far more vast and complex and marvelous than we had ever imagined. We are finding that even those voices we once heard as pagan and dangerous may speak an important part of Christ's truth to us.

And yet we know we can be seduced. We know that "right reason" can erode into self-serving rationalization. We know how hard the gospel can be, and how easy it is to lose our Easter joy by refusing the discipline and pain of our various Good Fridays. We need some simple limits to keep us from straying too far, and we try to make our creeds and catechism and single lines from scripture and traditional church teachings serve that purpose for us. Jesus said that there is only one way to God, and it is his way, the way he walked toward the cross. With all this debate going on, where is our road map now?

We wish sometimes for a massive instruction manual, and what we get instead is one another, eyes and ears and hands and feet of the body, the communion of saints throughout the ages, all different and all essential. Jesus is the way, but we have to walk it together. Jesus is the way, but the single central instruction is to love God and neighbor; and love seems to take the form of this peculiar Anglican curiosity, to find where Christ is in each of our odd companions, and to serve that Christ.

So discernment in these matters is not *primarily* meant to find answers, though that may happen with surprising ease when we stop trying to win an argument and start trying to seek and serve Christ in one another. Discernment searches for the lovely shape of Christ's body in this patient conversation among all those who have truths to tell. Some emphasize scripture, some tradition, some the power of their own experience; and all are needed. Maybe we will never agree on the specifics of sexual morality or much of anything else; but we might some day learn to trust the promise that we really are all one in Christ, called to live together in peace. Then we may also be brave enough to call one another to account, not just for breaking the rules, but for arrogance or rigidity or dishonesty or whatever else we discern to be harming the body itself.

Discernment of leaders for the church

Who will be the leaders for such a church? These days, nearly every diocese is struggling with the process by which we discern calls to ordained leadership. The word "discernment" is getting shopworn because of endless discussions of what it means and how we do it. Clearly, it is both necessary and presumptuous to take such authority over the direction of anyone's life.

For Episcopalians, the discussion has to start with our Baptismal Covenant, which designates every baptized person as a minister of the church. The baptismal service ends with a congregational welcome to the newly baptized, to "share with us in [Christ's] eternal priesthood." It would be a denial of baptismal grace to assume that bringing Christ's presence to the workplace or becoming a channel for God's love required ordination.

Baptism rests on the understanding that every person is called by God, and it enlists us in a lifelong process of discernment to discover the nature of our call. This is everybody's job, and a congregation that does it well may find leadership emerging all over the place, as people identify one another's gifts and offer guidance and support in using them. We need to be convinced that plumbers and lawyers and cooks and teachers and administrators and parents and flight attendants and security guards and home health aides can all be called by God to their particular service, and can further the kingdom by discerning how to do it with grace. People who know that will no longer see ordination as the only possible way to express their passion for ministry.

In fact, the baptismal promises call everyone who makes them to become not just a minister but in some sense a leader. Christians go forth into a world that is hardly ever eager to hear what Jesus has to say. Proclaiming the gospel, whether by word or by deed; serving Christ in all persons; striving for justice and peace—these are radical activities that are likely to set one apart from the crowd. Doing them effectively will probably require persuading others to join in, turning some folks in a different direction, and taking the risks of rejection and separation that go with leadership.

So the task of choosing ordained leaders is no longer a matter of looking for holy people, since holiness is shared by all. It can focus on identifying those who have demonstrated particular gifts for gathering and inspiring others, for articulating the faith, for living toward the promise of Easter when everything is falling apart. The process of discernment can in this way be somewhat demystified, since evidence of these gifts is often quite objective; and sometimes preference can go to those who meet particular needs of the church for specific ministries— for example among the poor or the young or those of diverse ethnic backgrounds.

But some mystery must always remain so that we will not miss the mavericks who fit none of the usual categories—the thorny prophets, the extraordinary people who are as difficult as Jesus and as surely chosen by God. The free movement of the Holy Spirit often takes us into the wilderness, and voices that come from there can sound as offensive and crazy as did John the Baptist's. Prayer can lessen our fear of them. Even with prayer God's choices will not always be confirmed by the church, but thanks to God's creativity, gifts for ministry need not be wasted just because a human institution does not know how to use them.

Discernment and mystery

Discernment, as we are coming to understand it, all but does away with the role of expert. It calls forth humility in even the wisest of us, and replaces the certainty of expertise with the wonder of seeking and finding Christ. This daily expectation of miracles turns discernment from burden to adventure and delight.

There is no part of our lives in which this gift is more wonderfully present than in the crises which leave even the most able of us helpless and lost. A stunningly competent woman is diagnosed with invasive cancer; a storybook family loses a child; a man of impeccable reputation is cracked open by an appalling mistake. "I don't know how to do this," they say, recognizing what less protected people may have known all along. Priests are called in as experts, but offer themselves instead as companions on a road that is new for every traveler. The most useful thing they can do is to remember that Christ is there too, and to join in looking for Christ's presence in every moment.

Building Up the Church

The work of discernment given us by our faith finds its richest regard exactly there, when all the old meanings collapse and what we have left is the assurance of Easter. Times like these strip us of platitudes, forbid the neat formulas of sin and punishment, and suspend us instead in the mystery of one morning when a few baffled and terrified people started learning that death doesn't win. Easter promises that after death comes new life, that even suffering holds the potential for joy, and we're invited to find it, to live it, even here, even now.

Here again, we are guided by the principles of Anglican discernment:

ONLY GOD IS GOD, and everything else can turn into an idol.

WE COULD BE WRONG, but that's forgivable.

And one more, which—if we were very lucky—embedded itself in our hearts when we were very young:

JESUS LOVES ME, THIS I KNOW.

Some of us learned it then with the simplicity of childhood, and we discover or return to it as hungry adults who are learning its meaning out of our need. It sustains all our work of discernment, and leaves us forgiven and free.

The Rev. Louise R. Conant
Associate Rector
Christ Church
Cambridge, Massachusetts

CHAPTER XIII

Spiritual Discernment

When you struggle with moral or ethical choices, wrestle with priorities, face personal problems or vocational questions, where do you turn for help? Do you ever think of looking to your parish community? Are the people who make up your congregation prepared to be channels of God's guidance to you? As the Body of Christ in a specific place, the parish can and should be able to offer such help.

To discern means to perceive, to distinguish, to recognize. Spiritual discernment is the endeavor to discriminate between the Spirit of God and other spirits around us, such as the spirit of competition, the spirit of a community or nation or decade (or even a congregation or denomination). These spirits are not necessarily bad, but we need to determine whether they are influencing us toward God or drawing us away. Another way of thinking about it is that we need to distinguish the voice of God from the other voices we hear. God can be speaking to us through the advice that friends and family give us, the TV programs we watch, and the things we read. Sometimes God speaks to us through voices we hear from our past, such as things that our parents or teachers used to say to us. Yet, these voices could be misguided, or we could apply good advice in the wrong way, thus misinterpreting God's will for us. The challenge is to sort out the various messages.

Throughout the history of the church, Christian communities have been centers of spiritual discernment. For Episcopalians today, the parish can be such a place. Certain qualities make a parish hospitable to discernment: an atmosphere of listening, an environment of humility, a sense of openness, the habit of reverence, a willingness to trust God, familiarity with scripture, and a knowledge of the signs of God's presence. These qualities must be developed and nurtured. It may be helpful to consider the contribution that each makes and to think about how to encourage its development.

Listening. If we want to hear what God has to say, we need to listen. In order to listen, we need to be quiet. The first thing to be done is to eliminate external sounds. Then we need to let the inner clatter simmer down—all those thoughts that race through our minds, mental restlessness, tensions that tighten our muscles.

Parishes can take practical measures to instill the habit of listening. One is to encourage church groups to begin their meetings—business meetings, committee meetings, classes—with a time for centering silence. By taking time to disengage from the bustle of their lives and become attuned to God's presence within themselves and among them, people can prepare to hear God and one another better. Because some people are uncomfortable with silence, it is advisable to propose the practice by explaining the rationale and taking time for discussion. To accommodate those who are unaccustomed to being quiet, it may be wise at first to try a short silence of only one or two minutes. Then, as people become acclimated, the length of the silence may be increased to five or ten minutes. To set the tone, the lights can be lowered for the time of silence. A candle or oil lamp burning at the middle of the room can have a quieting effect.

A second way a congregation can cultivate the habit of listening is to establish a parish-wide policy that asks people not to interrupt one another at parish-sponsored gatherings. If we interrupt others as they express themselves, it is a good indication that we are more interested in speaking than in listening. If "not interrupting" is established as a norm, everyone in the parish can help keep the groups in which they participate faithful to the practice.

Additionally, if we allow a deliberate, thoughtful pause after someone has spoken—whether in the normal dialogue of a class or meeting, or in formal speaking such as in a sermon—it allows an opportunity for us to absorb what has been said. A congregation that is serious about becoming a listening community can suggest that all parish groups encourage participants to pause between speakers. God speaks through people. As we learn to listen to one another, we learn to listen to God. Careful

Building Up the Church

listening requires constant attentiveness that can most effectively be cultivated in community. Genuine listening can have a transforming effect on a parish.

Humility. *Humility* is kin to the word humus—earth—and means down to earth. Humble people do not feel inferior; rather, they see themselves as incomplete except in relation to the whole of creation. Each person is unique and has something important to contribute, but every person and every group is minuscule compared to the greatness of God. No person and no group can know God's mind. The mystery is that as we recognize our own limits, God's wisdom can grow within us. Humble people, by definition, are not arrogant. Humility bestows a quiet confidence that comes through closeness to God and invites further closeness.

Openness. When we are open and honest with ourselves and with one another, we clear our vision to see the truth. As we recognize our own inadequacies and prejudices we are better able to hear what God has to say.

If people are going to articulate their thoughts and feelings honestly, the parish must be a safe place to do so. That means that members of the parish community must not criticize or belittle each other for what they think and feel. And, if something is spoken in confidence, it must not be repeated. When people dare to unmask themselves, they are better able to see through the eyes of God.

Reverence. Living with a sense of reverence for all of God's creation is a form of communicating with God. When we see God in every person we encounter, when we notice God's hand in the events and circumstances of our lives, when we seek God's compassion in what we do and say, we find God speaking to us in all aspects of our lives. The worship and education programs of a parish can be intentional about helping the congregation to experience the sacredness of all that is part of daily life.

Trust. In this culture, we are taught to be self-sufficient and encouraged to think that we can figure things out for ourselves. We are inclined to take things into our own hands and keep God on the margins. We want to plot our own paths and establish our own time-lines.

Trusting God does not imply abdicating responsibility. We need to apply our best resources—mental, physical, financial, and technological—to addressing our problems. But we need to hold our plans lightly so that God can shape them and perhaps even redirect them. The experience of trusting God demonstrates its worth, and that, in turn, reinforces our faith in God and makes it stronger. A parish can teach people to trust God by practicing such trust in its corporate life and helping people to experience it firsthand.

Scripture. God informs us through history, especially through the history of people who have tried to live their lives in close relationship with God. The Bible is a treasure house if we want to know God better and learn from the sacred stories recounted there. As we take the words of scripture into our prayer, God speaks to us anew to guide us in the situations of our daily lives. A congregation that consciously seeks God's guidance for its members individually and collectively must encourage individuals to read the Bible and must provide plentiful opportunities for Bible study and for reflection based on the Bible. As we become familiar with scripture and prayerfully apply it to our lives, we find the Holy Spirit giving direction to us in matters great and small.

Signs of God's Presence. Even after cultivating the conditions that give rise to discernment, we are left with the task of determining whether the things we hear are God speaking to us or not. We may not be sure immediately whether we are evaluating a situation accurately, but in hindsight we will likely know whether we did the right thing. There are certain signs that come from God that can help us weigh the evidence. The universal sign is peace. God's peace does not mean an absence of turmoil; it means wholeness and harmony, a serenity, a sense of confidence at the very deepest level, beneath any turbulence. Do not confuse the peace of God with a surface confidence, with superficial attempts at agreement, or with conformity born of weakness. Shallow, apparent peace will not survive the hard times; the peace of God endures through the ups and downs of life.

Among the signs of the Spirit are joy, energy, compassion, healing, unexpected fruitfulness, and the sudden coming together of various things that had been unfolding independently. When the opposite signs occur, it is an indication that we are probably on the wrong track. For instance, burnout is likely to be telling us that we are trying to do things for the wrong reasons—perhaps to meet the expectations of other people, to satisfy our ego needs, or to accommodate our own compulsions. It is important to look carefully to see what the signs are and to interpret them prayerfully.

Working at spiritual discernment does not give us a quick solution to every problem. It does help us walk more closely with God, which provides us with a better sense of the direction of the Spirit. Discernment is not simply a method, but a way of life that draws us into alignment with God's will. By intentionally seeking discernment, a parish can help its members develop a clearer sense of their paths in life and also help them see where the Spirit may be pointing in specific circumstances. Pursuing spiritual discernment can draw the people of a parish into a more intimate relationship with God and one another, making them more truly the Body of Christ.

Suzanne Farnum
Executive Director
Christian Vocation Project

Epilogue

The Lord did not command us to count his sheep but to feed them is the frequently heard rationale that defends the fact that a parish does not grow.

A question remains. Is the basic reason a parish does not grow because it does not want to grow? Growth, after all, means change and lack of stability and new possibilities. Do we seek a place of worship that provides one quiet center in the midst of this changing world?

That is not the world the Lord Jesus Christ died to give us. The world of Easter is a new world, different in every way from what we have known on earth. But the symbols and pale shadow of that new world are found here and now in the Body of Christ that we call the church. This Body, by definition, is a growing, changing, pulsing center of new life. And there are signs of this new life all around us, if we allow them to take root—and to grow.

Let us continue, therefore to join together in our common work to build up the church.